X Dup

Mexican American Identity

Mexican American Identity

Edited by Martha E. Bernal
and
Phylis C. Martinelli

La Mujer Latina Series
Giselle K. Cabello, Series Editor

Floricanto Press

La Mujer Latina Series

Copyright © 2005 by Floricanto Press

Copyright © 2005 of this edition by Floricanto Press

All rights reserved. Except for brief passages quoted in a review, no part of this book may be reproduced in any form, by photostat, microfilm, xeroraphy, electronic and digital reproduction, or placed in the Internet, or any other means, or incorporated into any information retrieval system, electronic, or mechanical, without written permission of the publisher.

ISBN: 0-915745-69-0

Floricanto Press
650 Castro Street, Suite 120-331
Mountain View, California 94041-2055
www.floricantopress.com

Table of Contents

Biogragraphical Sketches

Acknowledgments

Preface

Introduction:

1. Mexican American Identity: An Interdisciplinary Approach
   Phylis Cancilla Martinelli..19

Section I: Historical and Cross-Cultural Factors..................35

2. Mexican Immigrant Nationalism as an Origin of Identity for Mexican Americans: Exploring the Sources
F. Arturo Rosales...39

3. Expressive Ethnicity and Ethnic Identity in Mexico and Mexican America
John L. Aguilar..55

Section II: Children and Youths..69

4. The Young Mexican American Child's Understanding of Ethnic Identity
Martha E. Bernal, George P. Knight, Kurt C. Organista, Camille A. Garza, and Berlie M. Maez...75

5. Use of The Role/Identity Procedure for Assessing Ethnic Identity in Mexican American High School Students
Kurt C. Organista..93

Section III: Gender and Ethnic Identity................................111

6. Identity: Gender and Ethnic Dimensions
Patricia MacCorquodale..115

7. Dilemmas of the High Achieving Chicana: The Double Bind Factor in Male/Female Relationships
Judith Teresa González..141

Section IV: Social Policy..161

8. College Student Perceptions of Ethnic Identity: The case of Mexican Americans
Leonard Gordon..165

9. Ethnic Identity Research and Policy Implications for Mexican Americans
John A. García..179

Conclusion:

10. Theoretical Conceptualizations, Definitions, and Measurement of Ethnic Identity
Martha E. Bernal..195

BIOGRAPHICAL SKETCHES OF CONTRIBUTORS

John L. Aguilar is an associate professor of anthropology at Arizona State University. His research interests include social inequality, ethnicity, and social relations in rural Mexico and the American Southwest. He is co-author with Carlos Vallejo of "The 'culture' in bilingual/bicultural education." In E. García, F. Lomeli, and Y. Ortiz, (Eds.) Chicano studies: A multidisciplinary perspective (1984).

Martha E. Bernal has a joint appointment as professor in the Department of Psychology and research professor in the Hispanic Research Center at Arizona State University. Her research has dealt with the development and evaluation of parent training for conduct disordered children, minority mental health training, and ethnic identity in Mexican American children. She has served on the editorial boards of several journals, including Behavior Therapy, the Hispanic Journal of Behavioral Sciences, and the Journal of Social Issues. Her Ph.D. in clinical psychology is from Indiana University at Bloomington.

John A. García is associate professor and chair of the Dept. of Political Science at the University of Arizona at Tucson. His reseach focuses on the areas of political participation and its contributing factors and public policy. His most recent publication is "Hispanics and cancer preventive behavior: The development of a behavioral model and its policy implications." Journal of Health and Social Policy, 1, 1989.

Camille A. Garza completed her undergraduate studies at the University of Houston, and has received her M.A. in clinical psychology from Arizona State University where she continues work toward her Ph.D. In her dissertation she explores the effects of prejudice and discrimination on children's academic performance. Her research interests include stress and coping in ethnic minority children, and ethnic identity in Mexican American children.

Judith González is associate professor of women's studies at California State University, Fresno. Her main area of research focuses on health promotion and disease prevention among Hispanic women. A recent article is "Factors relating to frequency of breast self-examination among low-income Mexican American women." Cancer Nursing, 13, 1990.

Leonard Gordon is professor of sociology and associate dean in the College of Liberal Arts and Sciences at Arizona State University. His most recent article is "Race relations and attitudes at Arizona State University" in P. Althbach and K. Lomotey (Eds.), The racial crisis in American higher education (1991).

George P. Knight completed his Ph.D. in social/developmental psychology at the University of California at Riverside and then became an assistant professor at The University of Arizona. Currently he is an associate professor of psychology at the Dept. of Psychology at Arizona State University in Tempe, Arizona. He is a member of the editorial boards for Child Development and Merrill-Palmer Quarterly. His research interests include the development and socialization of ethnic identity, cross-cultural development, the development of prosocial and cooperative behavioral styles, and developmental social cognition.

Berlie López-Maez is a doctoral candidate in Counseling Psychology at Arizona State University. She works in private practice and in a psychiatric hospital in Phoenix. Her primary area of interest is in Mexican American studies. She is coauthor with J.E. Nanez and R. Padilla of "Bilingualism, Intelligence, and Cognitive Information Processing" in R. Padilla and A. Benavides (Eds.) <u>Critical Perspectives in Bilingual Education Research</u>.

Patricia MacCorquodale, associate professor of sociology, Univeristy of Arizona, specializes in the study of sex roles, ethnicity, human sexuality, women in science and math, and women's status cross-culturally. She is co-author with John DeLamater of <u>Premarital sexuality: Attitudes, relationships, and behavior</u>.

Phylis Cancilla Martinelli is assistant professor of sociology at St. Mary's College, Moraga, California. Her areas of interest are racial and ethnic studies and medical sociology. A recent publication is <u>Ethnicity in the sunbelt</u> (1989), New York: AMS Press. She is coeditor with Edward Murguia of a special issue on Latino identity in <u>Latino Studies Journal</u> (1991).

Kurt C. Organista is an assistant professor of social welfare at the University of California at Berkeley. His research interests center on the psychosocial adaptation of Chicanos/Latinos to the United States.

F. Arturo Rosales is an associate professor of history at Arizona State University. The focus of his research is Mexican Americans in the Southwest and Midwest; he has published several articles on this subject.

Mexican American Identity

Preface

This book presents a set of chapters which are based on working papers presented by the authors at the First Symposium on Ethnic Identity, held at Arizona State University in Tempe, Arizona, in the spring of 1987. The Symposium, entitled **Mexican American Identity: Conceptualization and Measurement in the Social Sciences**, was conceived as an oppportunity to gather a group of social scientists working on the ethnic identity of Southwestern Mexican Americans to discuss their views and work.

As indicated by the title of the conference, the aim of the organizers, Martha E. Bernal and Phylis C. Martinelli, was to address the questions, "How is ethnic identity conceptualized and measured by social scientists?" "What commonalities and differences exist among the scientists' approaches?" "Is it possible to arrive at some understanding of the nature of ethnic identity among social scientists?" The aim of this book is to provide some answers to these questions, and to offer some insights about ethnic identity from the perspectives of social scientists from different disciplines. This focus on ethnic identity reflects our view that it is a core explanatory construct in the understanding of the experience of ethnic minorities in the United States. Contact with the dominant Anglo American society inevitably leads to acculturation and to changes in cultural perspectives held by members of both immigrant and host cultures, but particularly by the former in the direction of assimilation to the latter. In immigrant and indigenous ethnic minority groups, this movement toward cultural assimilation is countered by numerous factors, including individual and group ethnic identity. Thus, while Mexican Americans may adopt English as a dominant language, and engage in many of the cultural ways and values of the Anglo, they may at the same time retain a strong identity as Mexican American. This identity may be the means by which they continue to perceive themselves as **different from** Anglo Americans as well as other ethnic groups, and by which they maintain cultural distinctiveness. It also influences their social behavior and interaction patterns. A concern with promoting the scientific understanding of this important construct was the overriding reason for the conference.

Both of us had been working on ethnic identity as a research topic for several years. It was Raymond Padilla, Director of the Hispanic Research Center at Arizona State University, however, who suggested that we organize the conference and hold it on our campus. And so we did, with the sponsorship and support of the Hispanic Research Center and the Graduate College, as well as with the cooperation of the Department of Psychology. Because the conference was well-received and attended, we decided to publish its proceedings. However, while chapters in this book are based on the Symposium papers, they have been substantially revised, and in addition they have been updated to include current literature. Furthermore, Phylis C. Martinelli has added a theoretical introductory chapter and Martha E. Bernal has added a concluding chapter that discusses and integrates the manner in which the interdisciplinary group of authors have conceptualized and measured ethnic identity.

Martha E. Bernal and Phylis C. Martinelli

_____*Mexican American Identity*_____

Introduction

Chapter I

Bernal and Martinelli

Mexican American Identity: An Interdisciplinary Approach

by

Phylis Cancilla Martinelli
St. Mary's College

This book focuses on ethnic identity, an important dimension of ethnicity for Mexican Americans who are one of America's major ethnic groups. Mexican Americans constituted 63% of the nation's Hispanics in the last decade (Bureau of the Census, 1986). Hispanics increased 50% between 1980 and 1990 to 22.3 million people, and collectively constitute 9% of the American population (McLeod, 1991). Projections estimate that the group will continue to increase to 19% percent of the total population by 2080 (Bureau of the Census, 1986).

Ethnic Identity

Given these demographic trends, it is essential to understand ethnic identity as it pertains to Mexican Americans since it has a wide ranging impact on both the individual and ethnic group (e.g., Dashefsky, 1976; De Vos & Romanucci-Ross, 1982; Royce, 1982). It forms a basic part of the personality of an ethnic person and is the basis of in-group social ties. Ethnic identity can influence a wide range of feelings for individuals, such as a sense of belonging and self-esteem or a sense of marginality and alienation. Ethnic identity can also influence a wide range of behaviors, including marital choices, friendship ties, patterns of seeking help, and voting preferences (e.g., Garza, 1981; Lovrich & Marenin, 1976; Miller, 1976). Furthermore, it is important in ethnic group formation and maintenance, with those having a high ethnic identity most likely to be concerned with issues of ethnic power and advancement (McKay & Lewins, 1978; Martinelli, 1986).

Ethnic identity is complex because it is not a fixed phenomenon; it can vary according to differing social conditions. Within a group it can vary across time and in relation to generation, social class position, occupation, religion, and the group's relation to the larger society (e.g., Dworkin, 1965; Gecas, 1973; Gordon & Mayer, 1983; Rutledge, 1985).

This last point deserves special attention. How the larger society reacts to an ethnic group's identity has a critical influence on both the present and the future of the group. This impact can be seen in several ways. The United States Census Bureau now offers persons of Spanish-speaking ancestry numerous choices in ethnic and racial identification (Lowry, 1982). The choices are eventually transformed into overall pictures of the various subgroups within the Hispanic population. These numbers and averages, in terms of socioeconomic, educational, and other demographic characteristics, influence the potential political power of the groups. They also influence the kind and amount of social services a group might receive, and the kind of attention gained in the media. Social policy orientations of the government toward non-English language use and immigration also affect an ethnic group since language is an important marker in defining in-group boundaries, and immigration renews the pool of members. The type of recognition that federal, state, and local governments give a group can also be influential. Being defined as an ethnic or racial minority means that a group can receive special protection from discrimination. Affirmative action guidelines and other mechanisms have been instituted to attempt to remedy past and continuing inequality for minorities.

Consequently, ethnic identity must be understood and measured. The following chapters represent varying scholarly views on this phenomena. Some are primarily theoretical while others provide a balance of theory and research. The topics covered include a historical analysis of Mexican American identity, longitudinal research on the core society's views of Mexican Americans and how these images can influence ethnic identity, research on the ethnic identity of Mexican American women, young children, and adolescents, and discussions of the political and policy impact

Mexican American Identity

of ethnic identity in cross-cultural and American settings.

Major Concepts

Ethnic identity is a complex subject. Inherent in most of the concepts relating to this topic are reciprocal concepts. Georg Simmel (Wolff, 1950) uses the term reciprocity to describe this occurrence in social life. Reciprocity focuses on the notion that certain social concepts always are balanced by other concepts. This balance can be seen in the basic concepts of ethnicity and identity. In Simmel's sense the term ethnic, derived from the Greek word **ethnos** that referred to outsiders or non-Greeks (Petersen, Novak, & Gleason, 1982), is reciprocal in relation to an insider or core group, which in American society has been the White Anglo Saxon Protestants. The term ethnic, by definition, carries implications for stratification since non-Greeks were by definition an inferior lot; barbarian meant non-Greek (Petersen et al., 1982). The term minority can describe any group that is in a subordinate position in the stratification system and is subjected to prejudice and discrimination by the majority group, or core group, in society. Some ethnic groups, such as Mexican Americans and African Americans, are also minority groups; the term minority ethnic group can be used for these groups. Some groups, such as Swedish Americans and German Americans, do not face prejudice and discrimination so they are not in a minority status; however, they have retained some cultural and identity distinctions that make them ethnic.

Similarly, identity has within it the notion of reciprocity, or balancing phenomenon. "Who am I?" is a basic human inquiry. This question is psychological in nature, with deep emotional roots, and immensely relevant to the individual. Yet, because of the individual's relation to society and social groups this question about the self must be framed in relation to other potential identities. Children, according to George Herbert Mead (1962), in order to develop a sense of self must learn to see themselves in relation to others. I am me means that I am not you; I am female means that I am not male.

There is also an inherent reciprocity between the group and the individual. The term ethnic requires recognition of the group since most definitions include the idea of shared characteristics. A useful definition of an ethnic group comes from Max Weber (1962). Weber states that ethnic groups are based on a subjective belief in a common ancestry. The belief in a common ancestry can be based on shared physical traits, culture, memories of emigration from a mother country or community, or memories of being colonized. This definition is useful in American society, since different groups have different ethnic bonds or markers. For example, some groups view race as their ethnic common bond, some stress an immigrant heritage or a refugee status, and others may claim several characteristics, including race and culture, as a common bond.

Views of Ethnic Identity

As the study of ethnicity has moved from industrialized nations to a global perspective, a variety of outlooks have developed on ethnic identity. These can be roughly divided into psychological or social psychological approaches and more sociological or anthropological approaches.

The psychological and social psychological approaches. These approaches tend to focus on ethnic identity as part of the personality structure (DeVos and Romanucci-Ross (1982). Researchers have examined what ego mechanism are involved in ethnic identification (Femminella, 1983), looked for patterns of behavior that can be termed ethnic personality (Devereux, 1982), and examined emotional reactions that may be typical of an ethnic group (Marsella, Murray, & Golden, 1974). The family is also examined for its role in shaping identity (Mindel & Habenstein, 1976), and shaping an ethnic world view (Novak, 1977).

Ethnic identity is also be viewed as part of a basic primordial attachment, acquired early in socialization, to the ethnic group (e.g., Keyes, 1981). From this view ethnic identity becomes an integral part of the ascribed self. It is so rooted in the basic personality that it is relatively unchangeable even with social mobility (Gordon, 1978). Thus, it is a powerful attachment because it fills the individual's need for a sense of collective continuity, providing a feeling of survival in an elemental psychological sense (DeVos, 1982). Because of the deeply rooted and often unexamined nature of ethnic identity at this psychological level it can be seen as potentially irrational.

A more social psychological orientation focuses on the relation between the individual and the "other" (DeVos & Romanucci-Ross, 1982; Rothman, 1965). This perspective examines the feelings of marginality that can arise within the ethnic individual who is often "...poised in psychological uncertainty between two (or more) social worlds..." (Stonequist, 1937). It also examines the impact of ethnic identity during various stages of the life cycle. For example, Kastenbaum (1979) points out that a child acquires ethnicity during part of their developmental process, that includes neurological, cognitive and interpersonal maturation. Later in life a person may try to erase ethnic attributes from his or her identity and thoughts, or at least examine these attributes from an adult perspective. However, ethnic characteristics may become resurgent during old age, and be particularly important for minority elderly (Maldonado, 1979).

Anthropological and sociological approaches. It can also be viewed as an essential factor in group formation. These approaches often note the rational aspects of ethnic identity in group mobilization and advancement. Fredrick Barth (1969) is known for his seminal work on ethnic boundaries. Barth notes that ethnic groups are basically a form of social organization with self-ascribed members an essential characteristic of the group. These members choose to identify with the group; they are not members simply because of having a social position determined by outsiders. Thus, individuals use their ethnic identities to draw social boundaries by which they classify themselves and others. The boundaries then become the basis for social interaction needed in the organizational formation of ethnic groups. These boundaries are symbolic elements epitomizing the cultural and social distinctiveness of "peoplehood."

Some researchers have investigated the use of ethnicity in vested group interests. For the person with an intense ethnic identity, or consciousness (McKay & Lewins, 1978), an ethnic trait(s) can be a very significant element of self-identity. The elementary feeling of solidarity found among such people often becomes translated into an "us versus them" orientation. Because of this polarization ethnic identity can be the basis for ethnic group conflict, social tension, and the mobilization of ethnic groups along political lines (e.g., Glazer & Moynihan, 1975; Patterson, 1977; Royce, 1982).

Still another view sees it as an important element in modern mass society. This perspective is a distinct contrast to those who predict the eradication of ethnicity in the modern age, and who view it as an archaic kind of affiliation that has no function in a contemporary, rational, rapidly changing environment (e.g., Geertz, 1968; van den Berghe, 1970). Theorists who see it as persisting despite modernization often see ethnic identity as a social anchor in an increasingly depersonalized and rapidly changing world (e.g., Fishman, 1983; Isajiw, 1975; Kinton, 1977). In some cases it fills the void left by the diminishing importance of religious and occupational identities (Glazier & Moynihan, 1970). In other instances, the ethnic group serves as a positive source of identity for ethnic minorities who face barriers to identification with a generic American identity.

Other theorists examine the more fluid aspects of situational ethnicity. This perspective suggests that ethnicity rarely encompasses the full range of an individual's social identities, and it may only be relevant in certain settings (Okamura, 1981; Yancey, Ericksen & Juliani, 1976). For example, a person's ethnic background may never be overtly discussed in a business setting, however, it may determine with whom one socializes after work. For the individual with an ethnic identity that is not a major part of self-identity, McKay and Lewins (1978) use the term ethnic awareness rather than ethnic consciousness. With ethnic awareness a person knows he or she possesses certain ethnic traits, but the traits are only one source of self-identity. Such awareness can result in interaction in ethnic organizations or in perceived membership in a broad social category so it does not mean ethnic ties are lost. Instead, ethnic ties and identity can be seen as diminished, and not the basis for an "us versus them" mentality.

A definition of ethnic identity. While there are obviously many views on the topic, a definition of ethnic identity and ethnicity that incorporates many of these perspectives is "... the character, quality, or condition of ethnic group membership, based on an identity with and/or a consciousness of group belonging that is differentiated from others by symbolic "markers"...and is rooted in bonds of a shared past and perceived ethnic interests." (Burgess, 1978).

Mexican American Identity

Mexican Americans can be defined, according to the above, as a minority ethnic group with a subjective belief in their common ancestry. The ethnic identity of Mexican Americans will be based, in part, on these definitions. Yet, within the Mexican American population is represented a wide range of experiences. These range from that of a recent immigrant living in an urban barrio or rural colonia to that of the middle-class, third generation person living in the suburbs. So, it can be expected that there will be variations on the central theme of Mexican American identity (Penalosa, 1970).

An example of this variation can be found with the choice of a term used to label this ethnic group. To begin to catalog the possible choices a person of Mexican ancestry can make in terms of an ethnic self-label is a formidable task. In choosing to use the term Mexican American throughout the chapters of this book the editors have, in fact, already entered into what has been called "the battle of the names" for Mexican Americans (Grebler, Moore, & Guzman 1970, p. 385). If ethnic identity is partly ascribed by the core group and partly chosen by ethnic group members then it is apparent that the label used to describe an ethnic person is important, and shaded with both psychological and political nuances. Researchers have identified an almost bewildering array of potential ethnic labels. These include Mexican, *mexicano*, Chicano, Mexican American, Pocho, Latin American, Spanish American, Latino/Hispanic, American of Mexican Descent, and American (García, 1981; Grebler et al., 1970; Hurtado & Arce, 1987). Actually this seemingly comprehensive listing does not include some of the regional identities that a Mexican American might choose such as Manito or Hispano if they were from New Mexico.

These various terms carry messages of either ethnic pride or distancing from the ethnic group. Three current debates emerge from these potential labels. The first relates to the use of the term Chicano. The origins of the term itself are debated (cf. Moore & Pachon, 1976; Ortego, 1973). However, in the social turmoil of the 1960s, whatever the original meaning, the term Chicano took on a new meaning with strong political connotations. Research has shown that those who identify as Chicano have clearly different identities than those who identify as Mexican American. Those who identify as Chicanos have stronger anti-Anglo feelings, coupled with a higher degree of anger, hostility, militancy, and an anti-establishment orientation, than those who identity as Mexican Americans (Lampe, 1978). Those with a Mexican American identity are more likely to feel positively toward integration, and to have a positive view of other ethnic groups (Lampe, 1978).

Some contend that the Chicano identity, despite fairly wide use in print, is not really favored by the majority of the Mexican American people but reflects a self-consciousness on the part of a small group of intellectuals (Connor, 1985). However, others argue that the use of the term by a highly educated elite may signal the beginning of a change that will gradually affect the larger Mexican American population (Hurtado & Arce, 1987). At any rate findings have shown considerable variation by nativity and language use in the choice of self-labels that reinforces the notion that Mexican Americans have a wide range of experiences (Hurtado & Arce, 1987).

The limited use of the label Chicano brings out a second point. It revolves around the fact that Mexican Americans are a mixed racial group, with both Native American and European Spanish ancestry, and some choose to emphasize one heritage above the other. A rejection of a general White identity based on choices of Mexican Americans for the 1980 census was observed by Hayes-Bautista and Chapa (1987). Other researchers claim that within the Mexican American community many reject identification with an Indian heritage, preferring an identity more closely aligned with a Spanish or European heritage (DeVos, 1982; Connor, 1985). In this respect, the term Chicano is linked to the Indian identity due to ties with the Brown Power movement and identification with La Raza.

The third debate is over the use of broad umbrella terms like Latino or Hispanic for ethnic self-identification. The use of a broad unifying term has some obvious instrumental implications. One positive side is that it can unify ethnic minority groups who have broad cultural and historical similarities (Totti, 1987). This unification has proven functional in advancing the political impact of Mexican Americans in some areas like Chicago, where they cooperated with Puerto Ricans (Padilla, 1984). However, even where it would be beneficial to use such terms in a multiethnic setting there is a current debate over whether the term Hispanic or Latino is more suitable (cf. Hayes-Bautista and Chapa 1987; Trevino 1987).

Nevertheless, despite some advantages, a pan-ethnic label, when used by policy makers, can obscure differences between various Hispanic groups, and present a picture of social improvement that does not totally reflect reality (Maldonado, 1985). The National Chicano Human Rights Council, a clearinghouse for information on Mexican Americans, has shown how statistics on Hispanics can obscure the problems of Mexican immigrants in America (Wurst, 1989). Another concern is that such terms do not really reflect the ethnic identity of Mexican Americans because they tend to dilute the uniqueness of that identity. Research by Hurtado and Arce (1987) has indicated that the use of generic terms like Hispanic and Latino are low for Mexican Americans, and tend to be used when speaking to those outside of their ethnic group.

A Theoretical Unity

With several branches of the social sciences represented in the following discussions of ethnic identity, it is difficult to isolate a common focus. While the chapters do not have a single theoretical focus, it is possible to identify either a direct or implied symbolic interaction approach in all of them.

Symbolic Interaction

Symbolic interaction refers to the way humans interact with each other through the use of symbols, such as language, cultural norms, and values (Mead, 1962; Blumer, 1969). A basic sense of self emerges out of interaction between the individual and society as the child begins to learn language. The use of language allows an important human characteristic to develop which is the ability to see oneself as an object, or as others see you. This process begins in the family, as the child develops a self-identity, and later learns the social roles associated with aspects of that identity. For example, a female child will learn that she is a girl, and what "good" and "bad" girls do. She will be able to see herself as "significant others," or those close to her, see her, and develop a sense of herself as good or bad. With maturation the child expands his or her behavioral references to the symbolic values and attitudes of "generalized other," or the larger community.

From a symbolic interactionist perspective ethnic identity is a variation on the central theme of self-identity. The ethnic child learns the basic symbols related to ethnicity from significant others. The child learns that he or she is Mexican American, and the symbolic attitudes, values, language, and behavior associated with that social role. If the child is raised in an ethnic community this group becomes the generalized other that helps the child develop a more mature sense of ethnic identity. However, the child also learns to interact with the symbolic definitions of their ethnic group that are held by the core community. The core community becomes another generalized other. From these dual generalized others may come conflicting symbols regarding ethnic identity. For example, the child may be praised at home and in the neighborhood for a good command of Spanish. In contrast, the reaction to Spanish proficiency from the core generalized other might range from indifference to a negative reaction. In establishing an ethnic identity the ethnic child must try to weigh the different symbolic interpretations of ethnic appearance, behavior, values, and attitudes, and his or her reaction to these different interpretations.

Ethnic identity can also be studied among adults. From the symbolic interaction perspective ethnic identity, once established, is not fixed or unchanging. Since people can choose to reinterpret symbolic meanings or to incorporate new symbols, ethnic identity can change for the individual across the developmental life cycle.

On a societal level symbolic interaction can also be used to understand groups or communities. Ethnic groups, like other groups, respond to symbols and form a collective identity. Mead (Cuzzort and King, 1976) saw history as important in establishing symbols needed for the group to establish its collective identity. The core group then serves as the generalized other for the ethnic group. As is the case with individuals, this ethnic group identity can change over time.

It may be possible to develop a comprehensive view of ethnic identity using symbolic interaction for a common theoretical orientation or in combination with other more structural perspectives. As Saenz and Aguirre (1988) note, there is "...a need for social psychological models of the self in ethnic studies" (p. 2). Like this author they see symbolic identity as a theoretical approach that offers the potential to provide such models. The purpose of such a unifying theory would be to provide a shared prespective that yields empirically testable propositions. An example of such a social psychological model is reference group theory that has provided stimulus for a wide range of empirical research (Merton, 1967).

Clearly, the time is critical for a more unified approach. As Mexican Americans and other Hispanics attempt to move toward a more egalitarian position in American society, in the manner of European ethnic groups, it is crucial to have a firm scientific understanding of their ethnic identity, since some important questions face social scientists. For example, as societal barriers to participation in the core group begin to drop, what will happen to Mexican Americans as an ethnic group? As marriages to those outside the ethnic group increase, how will people of mixed ancestry define themselves? Does the identity of one parent dominate, or can there be a dual ethnic identity? Does ethnic identity change according to the ethnic group one is with, or will ethnic identity disappear? Questions also remain for those of a single ethnic ancestry. With social acceptance, will ethnic identity for Mexican Americans become a largely meaningless vestige of an archaic tribalism that has no place in contemporary society (Alba, 1981; Steinberg, 1981)? Or will it continue to have relevance as a desirable social identity in a fast-paced, anomic modern society (Greeley, 1974)?

References

Alba, R. (1981). The twilight of ethnicity among American Catholics of European ancestry. The Annals, 454, 86-97.
Barth, F. (Ed.) (1969). Ethnic groups and boundaries. Boston: Little Brown.
Blumer, H. (1969). Symbolic interactionism: Perspective and method. Englewood Cliffs, New Jersey: Prentice-Hall.
Bureau of the Census (1986). Projections of the Hispanic population of the United States: 1983 to 2080. Series P-25, No. 995. Washington, DC: U.S. Government Printing Office.
Burgess, E. (1978). The resurgence of ethnicity: myth or reality? Ethnic and Racial Studies, 1, 265-285.
Connor, W. (1985). Who are the Mexican-Americans? A note on comparability. In W. Connor (Ed.), Mexican Americans in comparative perspective (pp. 2-28). Washington, D.C.: The Urban Institute.
Cooley, C. (1964). Human nature and the social order. New York: Schocken.
Cuzzort, R. P. & King, E. W. (1976). Humanity and modern social thought (2nd ed.). Hinsdale, Illinois: Dryden.
Dashefsky, A. (Ed.) (1976). Ethnic identity in society. Chicago: Rand McNally.
Devereux, G. (1982). Ethnic identity: Its logical foundations and its dysfunctions. In G. De Vos & L. Romanucci-Ross (Eds.). Ethnic identity, cultural continuities and changes (2nd ed., pp. 42-70). Chicago: University of Chicago Press.
DeVos, G. (1982). Ethnic pluralism: conflict and accommodation. In G. DeVos & L. Romanucci-Ross (Eds.). Ethnic identity, cultural continuities and change (2nd ed., pp. 5-41). Chicago: University of Chicago Press.
DeVos, G. & L. Romanucci-Ross (Eds.) (1982). Ethnic identity, cultural continuities and change (2nd ed.). Chicago: University of Chicago Press.
Dworkin, A. G. (1965). Stereotypes and self-images held by native-born and foreign-born Mexican Americans. Sociology and Social Research, 49, 214-224.
Femminella, F. (1983). The ethnic ideological themes of Italian Americans. In R. Juliani (Ed.), The family and community life of Italian Americans (pp. 109-120). New York: American Italian Historical Association.
Fishman, J. (1983). Language and ethnicity in bilingual education. In W. Mc Cready (Ed.) Culture, ethnicity, and identity (pp. 127-137). New York: Academic.
García, J. (1981). Yo soy Mexicano...self-identity and sociodemographic correlates. Social Science Quarterly, 62, 88-98.
Garza, M. (1981). Ethnic identity and mental health status: Formal and informal help seeking resources of Chicanos, a comparative study. (Doctoral dissertation, Michigan State University, 1981). Dissertation Abstracts International, 42, 3758A.
Gecas, V. (1973). Self-conceptions of migrants and settled Mexican Americans. Social Science Quarterly, 54, 579-95.
Geertz, C. (1968). The integrative revolution: Primordial sentiments and civil politics in the new states. In C. Geertz (Ed.), Old societies and new states (pp. 105-157). New York: The Free Press.
Glazier, N. & Moynihan, D. (1970). Beyond the melting pot: Negroes, Puerto Ricans, Jews, Italians, and Irish of New York City. Cambridge: MIT Press.

Glazier, N. & Moynihan, D. (Eds.) (1975). Ethnicity: Theory and experience. Cambridge: Harvard University Press.

Gordon, M. (1978). Human nature, class, and ethnicity. New York: Oxford.

Gordon, L. & Mayer, A. (1983). The effects of U. S. generation on religio-ethnic identity: Evidence from the national Jewish population survey. Humboldt Journal of Social Relations, 10, 143-162.

Grebler, L. J. Moore, & Guzman, R. (1970). The Mexican American people. New York: The Free Press.

Greeley, A. (1974). Ethnicity in the United States. New York: John Wiley.

Hayes-Bautista, D. & Chapa, J. (1987). Latino terminology: Conceptual basis for standardized terminology. American Journal of Public Health, 77, 61-67.

Hurtado, A. & Arce, C. (1987). Mexicans, Chicanos, Mexican Americans, or Pochos...que somos? Aztlan, 17, 103-130.

Isajiw, W. (1975). The process of maintenance of ethnic identity: The Canadian context. In P. Mingus (Ed.), Sounds Canadian: Languages and cultures in multi ethnic society (pp. 129-139). Toronto: Peter Martin.

Kastenbaum, R. (1979). Reflections on old age, ethnicity, and death. In D. Gelfand & A. Kutzik (Eds.), Ethnicity and aging (pp. 175-183). New York: Springer.

Keyes, C. (Ed.) (1981). Ethnic change. Seattle: University of Washington Press.

Kinton, J. (Ed.). (1977). America's ethnic revival: Group pluralism entering America's third century. Aurora, Ill: Social Science and Sociological Resources.

Lampe, P. (1978). Ethnic self-referent and the assimilation of Mexican Americans. International Journal of Comparative Sociology, 19, 259-270.

Lovrich, N. & Marenin, O. (1976). A comparison of Black and Mexican voters in Denver. Western Political Quarterly, 29, 285-297.

Lowry, I. (1982). The science and politics of ethnic enumeration. In W. Van Horne & T. Tonnesen (Eds.), Ethnicity and public policy (Vol 1., pp.42-61). Milwaukee: University of Wisconsin System.

McKay, J. & Lewins, F. (1978). Ethnicity and the ethnic group: A conceptual analysis and reformulation. Ethnic and Racial Studies, 1, 412-427.

McLeod, Ramon G. (1991, March 12). Hispanic population doubles since 1980. San Francisco Chronicle. p. A 3.

Maldonado, Jr. D. (1979). Aging in the Chicano context. In D. Gelfand & A. Kutzik (Eds.) Ethnicity and aging (pp. 175-183). New York: Springer.

Maldonado, L. (1985). Altered states: Chicanos in the labor force. In W. Van Horne & T. Tonnesen (Eds.), Ethnicity and the work force (Vol IV, pp.145-166). Milwaukee: University of Wisconsin System.

Marsella, A., Murray, M. & Golden, C. (1974). Ethnic variations in the phenomenology of emotions: Shame. Journal of Cross-Cultural Psychology, 5, 312-329.

Martinelli P. (1986). A test of the McKay and Lewins typology. Ethnic and Racial Studies, 9, 196-210.

Mead, G. H. (1962). Mind, self, & society. Chicago: University of Chicago Press.

Merton, R. (1967). On theoretical sociology. New York: The Free Press.

Miller, M. V. (1976). Mexican Americans, Chicanos, and others: Ethnic self-identification and selected social attitudes of rural Texas youths. Rural Sociology, 41, 234-237.

Mindel, C. & Habenstein, R. (Eds.) (1976). Ethnic families in America: Patterns and variations. New York: Elsevier.

Moore, J. & Pachon, J. (1976). Mexican Americans (2nd ed.). Englewood Cliffs, NJ: Prentice-Hall.

Novak, M. (1977). Further reflections on ethnicity. Middletown, Pa: Jednota Press.
Okamura, J. (1981). Situational ethnicity. Ethnic and Racial Studies, 1, 452-465.
Ortego, P. (Ed.) (1973). We are Chicanos: An anthology of Mexican American literature. New York: Washington Square Press.
Padilla, F. (1984). On the nature of Latino ethnicity. Social Science Quarterly, 65, 651-664.
Patterson, O. (1977). Ethnic chauvinism: The reactionary impulse. New York: Stein and Day.
Peñalosa, F. (1970). Toward an operational definition of the Mexican American. Aztlan, 1, 1-12.
Petersen, W., Novak, M. & Gleason, P. (1982). Concepts of ethnicity. Cambridge, Mass: Belknap.
Rothman, J. (1965). Minority group identification and inter-group relations. Chicago: Research Institute for Group Work in Jewish Agencies.
Royce, A. (1982). Ethnic identity: Strategies of diversity. Bloomington, Indiana: Indiana University Press.
Rutledge, P. (1985). The role of religion in ethnic self-identity: A Vietnamese community. New York: University Press of America.
Saenz, R. & Aguirre, B. E. (1988, August). Mexican descent and ethnic identity. Paper presented at the meetings of the American Sociological Association, Atlanta, GA.
Steinberg, S. (1981). The ethnic myth: Race, ethnicity, and class in America. New York: Antheneum.
Stonequist, E. (1937). The marginal man. New York: Charles Scribner's Sons.
Totti, X. (1987). The making of a Latino ethnic identity. Dissent, 34, 536-42.
Treviño, F. (1987). Standardized terminology for Hispanic populations. American Journal of Public Health, 77, 69-71.
Van den Berghe, P. (1970). Race and ethnicity. New York: Basic Books.
Weber, M. (1965). Ethnic groups. In T. Parsons (Ed.), Theories of society, foundations of modern sociological theory (Vol 1, pp. 305-309). New York: The Free Press.
Wolff, K. (1950). The sociology of Georg Simmel. New York: The Free Press.
Wurst, R. (1989, February 2). Message on Chicano identity. The San Ramon Valley Times, p. 8A.
Yancey, W., Ericksen, E. & Juliani, R. (1976). Emergent ethnicity: A review and reformulation. American Sociological Review, 3, 391-394.

Bernal and Martinelli

Mexican American Identity

Section I

Bernal and Martinelli

Mexican American Identity

Section I

Historical and Cross-Cultural Factors

The first articles serve to place Mexican American ethnic identity in a broad context beyond the borders of the United States and into an earlier time frame. By moving both back in time and geographically into other nations the discussion of ethnic identity for Mexican Americans gains added substance. One can see how some of the issues raised in the Introduction, for example, the conflict between an Indian identity and a European identity, are not limited to contemporary Mexican Americans but have roots in a divided ethnicity based in Mexico.

Evolution of Contemporary Identities

Arturo Rosales in his chapter on the history of Mexican American ethnic identity in the United States shows the evolution of many of the contemporary identities that contribute to today's "battle of the names." The chapter delineates the two important sources for ethnic identity. The first is the regional identity associated with natives of the Southwest areas conquered by the Spanish. The second, and perhaps the most important identity according to Rosales, is an immigrant identity that emerged in the 1890s in the *colonias* of American cities and continued to grow in this century. Through a thoughtful discussion of scholarly debates on the development of these identities he shows similarities and differences to the ethnic identity of White ethnics, like Italian and Jewish Americans, and Mexican Americans.

Rosales shows how structural factors in the country of origin and in American society have influenced the ethnic identity of Mexican Americans. He focuses on dominant and minority group relationships by tracing the influence of Anglo society on the two self-identities that develop for Mexican Americans. Most immigrants from Mexico arrive in

America with a weak sense of a national Mexican identity. However, the negative treatment that immigrants receive in America began to forge a Mexican American ethnic identity, and this ethnic identity proved important in group survival. This identity stressed loyalty to Mexico and Mexican culture; a "*Mexico Lindo*" (Beautiful Mexico) mentality prevailed.

Indian and Ladino Identities

John Aguilar's work draws attention to complex theoretical issues in ethnic identity. He focuses his research on Mexico and demonstrates that there is not a monolithic Mexican national identity. Instead, Indian communities often have distinct ethnic identities from Ladinos (non-Indian Mexicans). Thus, Mexicans can be part of stratified ethnic relationships similar to the experience of Mexican Americans in the United States.

Aguilar notes that ethnic identity is a resource for both the individual and the group. For the individual, ethnic identity can enhance a feeling of self-worth, and he suggests that this important psychological dimension needs to be incorporated in political and economic perspectives on ethnicity. For the ethnic group, the expressive, or psychological, dimension of ethnicity is also important. Ethnic leaders can mobilize fellow ethnics more easily if their emotional attachment to ethnic symbols, their feelings of ethnic pride, and their feelings of hostility toward the core group can be activated.

Chapter 2: Mexican immigrant nationalism as an origin of identity for Mexican Americans: Exploring the sources. F. A. Rosales.

Chapter 3: Expressive ethnicity and ethnic identity in Mexico and Mexican America. J. L. Aguilar.

Chapter II

Mexican Immigrant Nationalism As An Origin Of Identity for Mexican Americans: Exploring The Sources

by

F. Arturo Rosales
Arizona State University

Tracing Mexican American ethnic identity would appear a most difficult task because of the seemingly confusing maze of self identifiers which Mexican Americans have used historically, such as *californios, tejanos, mexicanos*, Latin Americans, Spanish, Mexican Americans, Chicanos and Hispanics. Mexican Americans have even distinguished those Mexicans that are seen as different from themselves, irrespective of how slight the difference might appear to non-Mexicans. For example, *cholo, surumato, guacho*, or *mojado* serve to identify those who have recently arrived from Mexico. In the 1920s, in fact, the word Chicano was used to denote new arrivals also. Mexicans who have their origin in Mexico, on the other hand, coined the terms *pocho* referring to second generation Mexican Americans, and *manito* to describe the Mexicans who have been in northern New Mexico and southern Colorado since the 17th century.

The numerous identifiers introduced above, however, represent changing attitiudes and prejudices and different epochs in history as new terms replaced those that no longer seemed relevant. The contention of this paper is that there are only two major sources on which ethnic identity is built. One source is that of being a foreigner in Anglo America and shaping an identity occurs around that perception, as it does with all other immigrants who arrived after Anglo American core culture became firmly entrenched in the 19th century. There is, however, among many Chicano intellectuals, resistance to the idea that the experience of Mexicans in the United States is like that of other immigrants. Such scholars as Alfredo Mirande (1987) and John R. Chavez (1984) believe that since Mexicans have been in the Southwest longer than Anglos, they have a similar claim to the land as the American Indian. Or as Chavez asserts, they identify with the "lost land." He makes a strong case for the idea that Mexicans identify with the heritage of the old Hispanic Southwest. According to Chavez, Mexicans who lived in the extreme Mexican (now the Southwest) north during the early 19th century intimately identified with the land, the flora, and the fauna. Mirande succinctly presents this same image in the following passage:

> Chicanos strongly resist the notion that they are somewhat transplanted or imported 'immigrants.' Not only has The Chicano been in America for a long time but...they did not come to the United States, rather, the United States came to them (p.101).

Chavez also asserts that links with Mexico, the nation, were weak, and since immense geographical distances separated regions in the extreme north, the inhabitants did not identify with each other. Consequently, natives of Hispanic coastal California called themselves *californios, tejanos* was used by inhabitants of the Lower Rio Grande Valley, while in the Upper Rio Grande, Hispanic natives called themselves *mexicanos* derived from Nuevo Mexico, not from identification with Mexico. Then within the actual regions, class divisions existed, but as Southwest Mexicans felt the brunt of Anglo domination after the takeover they acquired a stronger sense of ethnic cohesion (Chavez, 1984).

There is no doubt that this notion can be applied to the 80 to 100,000 Mexican people at mid-19th century when the United States took it over. How these people felt about themselves, especially as they responded to Anglo American political and cultural domination, is crucial to understanding the evolution of Mexican American identity.

Corroborating this notion is Robert Rosenbaum (1981) who, speaking of the rise of Hispanic resistance to Anglo domination in the Southwest, states that before the takeover by the United States: "After family relationships, regional affiliations provided the strongest lines of association among *mexicanos*". But "As Anglo pressure increased during the 19th and into the 20th century, race, religion, and custom rose in importance as foci for social alliances" (p. 10). Similarly, Richard Griswold del Castillo (1979, pp. 103-105) sees increasing anti-Mexican violence as responsible for the rise of ethnic consciousness among *Californios*. Even the elite *Californio* leaders who initially sided with Anglo Americans against banditry started identifying with Mexican social bandits in California during the late 19th century. As Anglo America advanced its hegemony, distinctions were blurred as a new communication system integrated the Southwest, and Anglo oppression leveled Mexican American *ricos* into the proletariat class made up of both immigrants and lower class natives (Griswold del Castillo, 1979, pp. 103-105).

Notwithstanding the "lost land" influence, the contention in this paper is that the main source of image building for Mexican Americans came out of the immigrant *colonias* which mushroomed in the United States throughout the last decade of the 19th century and which still continue to grow. Native Southwest identity traits, which have a much longer tenure in the United States Southwest than those of Anglos, were important in influencing the identity of incoming immigrants only where a residue of old Hispanic culture remained strong, as in south Texas, southern New Mexico and southern Arizona. Ironically, few immigrants from Mexico settled where traditional southwestern culture was even stronger, in northern New Mexico and southern Colorado.

When immigrants from northern Sonora or northern Coahuila would immigrate into the adjacent states on this side of the border, they would find that culture, climate, and economy were the same as in their home areas. For a person from Guanajuato or Vera Cruz, however, working in commercial agriculture in the Southwest, in 100 plus degree weather contrasted radically to the temperate climate and more preindustrial working conditions which were left behind in Mexico (Anguiano, 1974; Hernandez, 1974).

In making a case for the relevancy of the "Lost Land" identity for all Chicanos, regardless of whether their origins are immigrant or native Southwest, Mirande (1987) notes that "although Chicanos are a landless people...barrios are a symbolic land base and an important source of identity and pride" (p. 26). But certainly there is plenty of evidence to demonstrate that other immigrant groups find that same source of identity from their ethnic neighborhoods. But this paper does not intend to disprove the connection which Mexicans have to what used to be northern Mexico. Instead, the purpose is to identify the very close connection which most Mexican Americans have to Mexico, a nation that they see as the "Old Country." This is an experience which only immigrants who find themselves in a foreign land can have. To suggest otherwise, as Mirande (1987) does, in many respects denies the heritage and struggle which the Mexican immigrants have undergone in the United States in order to survive and adapt.

By the 1920s, the majority of the immigrant *colonias* were in cities like Houston, Dallas, Chicago, and Phoenix which were built by Anglos, and where Mexican immigrants found few familiar surroundings. Or as was the case in Los Angeles, the Anglo expansion of the city rendered the old Hispanic core a faint vestige of its Mexican Hispanic past. In addition, by this time the vast majority of persons living in the United States who were considered of Mexican origin were either born in Mexico or the children of immigrants.

In some instances, when native Hispanics mixed with immigrants in areas to which both groups were drawn to work, such as in Northeastern Colorado, conflict resulted. Native Southwest Mexicans distinguished themselves from Mexican immigrants by using epithets such as *cholos*, *surumatos*, or *guachos* to describe the newcomers. Eventually, the original antipathy gave way to grudging acceptance of marriages and other social liaisons. After all, both groups possessed more similarities than differences in matters of race, religion, language, and custom (Taylor, 1929, pp. 212-116).

The "Lost Land" legacy then, has to be considered in a combined fashion with the immigrant source of identity to determine respective contributions to the evolution of Mexican American identity. Ironically, while Southwest Hispanics applied epithets to Mexican immigrants, regardless of where they came from, the immigrants themselves did not necessarily identify with each other either. Like other newcomers to the United States in the late 19th and early 20th century, Mexicans came from a peasant or an agricultural village background and were from a part of the world which was barely acquiring a sense of nationhood. An extensive *patria chica* (small homeland) identity existed among the majority of the immigrants as they left for the United States.

According to Henry C. Schmidt (1978) at the beginning of the national period, or early 19th century, in Mexico "...a sense of national identity was by no means well developed or widespread. The term *Mexican* might refer to a region or locale, but never to a nation" (p. 19).

Then, throughout the 19th century, liberal vs. conservative, Indian-Mestizo vs. Spanish muddled the idea of national identity. Schmidt (1978) further asserts that shape had to come from abroad. Positivism, a philosophy with virulent anti-Indian strains during the late 19th century Porfiriato, removed the idea of national identity from the ignored and sometime despised masses, according to Schmidt's line of reasoning (pp. 21-35). Frederick Turner (1968) and John J. Johnson (1965) in their studies on the rise of nationalism in Latin America go even further. Turner claims nationalism is most conspicuous by its absence in 19th century Mexico and Johnson states that not until 1925 does nationalism appear anywhere in Latin America (cited in Sinkin, 1979, pp. 147-148). Richard A. Sinkin (1979, pp. 147-148) writing on the rise of a nation during the Benito Juarez era, from the 1850s to the 1870s, does not agree completely with any of these contentions and offers a more balanced interpretation. The former theories do not differentiate between the provincial masses and the more astute political elites, according to Sinkin. The elites had achieved a consciousness with the constant interfering of outside powers, such as the invasions by the United States in 1846 and France in 1862. In essence, the nation building process apparent during this period did create a sense of nationalism, although it was concentrated in the more urban sectors of Mexican society. But even accepting this view of the development of limited nationalism, we have to conclude that since the majority of the immigrants who came to the United States were from the provincial regions, and not from the upper classes, they would carry very little of this sentiment with them.

For example, Luis Gonzalez (1972) in his classic study of San Jose de Gracia, a village located in the heavy immigrant-sending region of northern Michoacan states:

> We can be sure that those who lived here before 1861 knew each other very well but had hardly any knowledge of human beings or events anywhere else....At the turn of the twentieth century not much had changed. On the eve of the revolution their lives were beginning to be affected by nationalistic sentiment, an interest in politics and an awareness of the outside world, curiosity about new inventions and a desire to make money....The better informed citizens knew who Don Porfirio Diaz, Aristeo Mercado and the prefects of Jiquilpan were; but the majority were unaware of the move toward

nationalism, or even toward regionalization (Gonzalez, p. 112).

That many future immigrants did not identify with Mexico as a nation as late as the 1920s is vividly demonstrated by the religious wars taking place in Mexico during that decade. Paul S. Taylor (1933), who researched numerous *colonias* throughout the United States in the 1920s, also studied Arandas, Jalisco which, like San Jose de Gracia, was another typical immigrant sending community in West Central Mexico. He describes the residents of the village as sharing neither the desire for agrarian reforms, nor the anticlericalism of the Mexican revolutionaries. When confronted with both of those issues in the 1920s, the villagers sided overwhelmingly with the dramatic reaction to anti-clericalism, the Cristero rebellion.

Los Altos of Jalisco, where Arandas is located, shared with numerous other communities in West Central Mexico many common characteristics. The religious schism expressed in Arandas is representative of attitudes carried to the United States by thousands of immigrants because West Central Mexico was the largest single source of Mexican immigration to the United States. If loyalties there ever transcended *patria chica* boundaries, they extended towards a spiritual rather than a political entity. Taylor (1933) succinctly provides evidence for this in quotation which demonstrates the degree to which Arandas residents identified with their religion: "Our religion is twenty centuries old, and cannot be killed. If you lose today, tomorrow you will win. The Soul is all over, and the religious are always right (p. 38)."

As a consequence, Mexicans did not arrive in the United States with the solid group cohesion that was more characteristic of some immigrant groups such as Jews. Because of such unity, this latter group made relatively quicker and easier transitions to life in the new home than other immigrants. Eastern European Jews, for example, who left their homeland because of political persecution at the turn of the century, knew that they would never go home. This irrevocable commitment to staying in this country led to a quick and decisive response to adverse conditions.

In addition, Jews arrived in the United States with a stronger sense of cohesion and ethnic identity than most other immigrant groups, a sense that was acquired in urban settings back in their homelands. They also came prepared with the tools for maintaining unity, such as a common language (Yiddish), theater and literary traditions, and a religion which encouraged intellectual participation and emphasized cultural nationalism.

Mexican American Identity

In essence they identified with each other, regardless of whether they came from Poland or the Russian Pale (Jones, 1960, pp. 200-201; Olson, 1979, 274-275).

Mexicans had more in common with New Immigrants like Italians and Eastern Europeans. In the initial immigrant settlements, friends and relatives from the same village or province in the old country lived and socialized together, forming parochial clusters within the larger enclave, a phenomenon that anthropologists call primordial cohesiveness. Often the immigrants would physically segregate themselves in sections of *barrios* which would eventually acquire names like *El Michoacanito* or *Chihuahita*. In addition, some of the ethnic organizations would have a preponderance of members who originated in the same province of Mexico. Divisions based on regional origins and religious schisms were further complicated by significant class differences. Even though the vast majority of the Mexicans in the United States were from the "*gente humilde*" (lower classes), many "*gente decente*," (upper and middle class refugees) did join them in the immigrant *colonias* (Anguiano 1974; García, 1981, p. 262; Rosales, 1976, p. 196).

Very early in the formation of the immigrant *colonias*, however, Mexicans acquired an exalted form of immigrant nationalism. The majority of the Mexicans entering the United States between 1910 and 1930 were seeking work, not refuge. Many returned home, but even those who never did, harbored a dream of someday going back. Consequently, the immigrant *colonias* looked towards Mexico during this era, a condition reflected in their orientation. Another characteristic of this emerging identity was an exaggerated loyalty to Mexico coupled with a dutiful celebration of the Mexican patriotic holidays (*Fiestas Patrias*). In short, a "*Mexico Lindo* (Beautiful Mexico)" mentality absorbed the identity of the *colonias*.

Consider for instance, a passage from *El Amigo del Hogar*, (April 17, 1927), a newspaper printed in the East Chicago, Indiana *colonia* during the 1920s. "We must take from this country where we are not respected the best so that when we return to the homeland we can contribute to our nation's development" (Translation by Author). Published by a conservative refugee who had been a government official in Mexico, the statement sums up an overriding sentiment held by immigrant leaders wherever they lived.

But considering that historical evidence demonstrates that on the eve of large scale immigration, nationalism was very poorly developed in immigrant sending areas of Mexico, why was it evident in the Mexican *colonias* almost immediately? One answer to this seemingly paradoxical question is that the emotions associated with devotion and allegiance to the homeland were acquired in the United States by thousands of immigrants, who heretofore possessed a *patria chica* world view. Taylor (1930) noted that in South Texas "Mexican citizens in the United States are very patriotic, with...an exaggerated patriotism of the reluctant expatriate" (p. 367). He also made a similar observation in Chicago. "First there is a strong emotional attachment to Mexico and patriotism is heightened, as the Mexicans themselves sometimes note, by their expatriation" (Taylor, 1932, p. 215).

An editorial appearing in *La Prensa* of San Antonio during the 1920s echoed this feeling. "They [the Mexicans] know that patriotism augments and increases" in the United States (quoted in Taylor, 1932, p. 115). Taylor (1932) interviewed another Mexican who told him, "The Mexicans become patriotic here and they want to celebrate but they don't even know the Mexican national hymn" (p.115). A vehicle had to exist, however, for bringing nationalist ideology into the United States. During the Mexican Revolution, a sizeable portion of the Mexican urban middle classes and elites, whom Sinkin indicated were the critical core in Mexico imbued with nationalistic feelings, immigrated to the United States. They were the most important source of nationalism, in addition to being the carriers of *indigenismo* (pride in the Indian heritage of Mexico), and other forms of patriotism.

But what blueprint did the Mexicans use as they established their ethnic identity in the United States? The maintenance of Spanish was seen as the most necessary nationalist statement. In 1928, *La Sociedad Benito Juarez* started a Spanish language school in order that the Mexican children in Houston would "retain the Language of their homeland" (Rosales, 1981, p. 236). In addition, naturalization was discouraged by immigrant leaders, and the main political concerns were those associated with Mexico.

Also during this time, *indigenismo* was central to ethnic identity among Mexican immigrants. This ideology was deeply rooted in Mexican history, given profound expression by Mexican intellectuals and writers in the colonial era and throughout most of the nineteenth century. Even though, after Mexico's independence, it was rejected by European style liberals whose ideas were the basis for the Positivistic ideological orientation of the *porfiriato, indigenismo* always had a strong appeal to provincial history buffs, school teachers, and since the cult of the Virgin of

Mexican American Identity

Guadalupe was central to the ideology, to ardent Catholics. Able to survive the Positivistic assault during the Mexican Revolution, because of its grassroots adherence, *indigenismo* was resurrected by revolutionary intellectuals (Brading, 1973; see Schmidt, 1978 for a discussion of *indigenismo*)

The ideology had widespread appeal and was embraced by Mexicans regardless of their political preferences. Understandably, the sentiment was carried to *colonias* in the United States by immigrant leaders who deliberately maintained and projected this image.

In an essay in *El Amigo del Hogar* (December 13, 1925), for example, the editor and publisher shows an identification with the Indian past in a homage to the Virgin of Guadalupe.

> ...since our Brown Virgin left her image on Juan Diego's cloak the Indian, the oppressed, have been transformed; he was able to gain strength and raise the sacred banner of independence which gave him a nation and freedom....The dream was sustained by the memory that through his veins ran the blood of heroes, of Cuauhtemoc who defiantly endured torture by the Spaniards. We were a race of eagles in forced impoverishment and titans bound by the chains of oppression.

In Houston, Texas, Mexicans also proudly recognized their Mestizo-Indian heritage. For example, the *Acta Primordial* (1919) of la *Sociedad Benito Juarez* provides a direct indication that Houston Mexicans were proud of their Indian heritage. According to the document, founding members received the announcement that the organization would be named after Mexico's most distinguished political leader with a standing ovation and: ...every one declared that all Mexicans love and identify with this pure Indian who through personal hard work and civic virtues rose to the highest honor afforded his compatriots, becoming a symbol of Mexican nationalism.

Another poignant appeal to racial pride also appeared in *Gaceta Mexicana* during the 1920s. Written by Houston jeweler, Emilio R. Ypina, it was entitled "We the Indians "(May 15, 1928). It begins by decrying one Spanish historical source which depicts Benito Juarez in the following manner. "He was of the Indian race BUT he was intelligent and good willed." Ypina goes on to berate the authors of the reference for ignoring all of the technological, cultural and philosophical achievements of "...our Indian Fathers....Or do they think that we their children also need a 'but' to be considered intelligent and goodwilled?" (Translation of last three quotations by author).

In spite of the parochial outlook of lower class immigrants, it was not difficult for the more sophisticated leaders to influence them, because accompanying all of the newly arriving Mexican immigrants were homogeneous cultural traits that made it obvious that they were from the same Mexican background. They spoke Spanish, racially they were similar, and the vast majority were Catholic. In his studies of ethnicity in the United States, Timothy L. Smith (1978) has demonstrated that religious affiliations carried over from the old country provided the basis for transcending the initial parochial outlook of the immigrant communities and contributing to the formation of ethnic consciousness. Considering the above factors we can conclude that newcomers from the "gente humilde" would readily identify with the cultural and nationalistic symbols which the elites offered them. Because of the widespread appeal of this symbolism, this class was drawn very quickly to the process.

But why would the class of *"gente decente"* bother to unite with an element that back in Mexico they would have avoided? John Bodnar (1973, pp. 309-330) who like Timothy L. Smith (1978) is in the forefront of studying the formation of ethnic consciousness among immigrants in the United States, concludes that adverse conditions encountered by the immigrants in their new home contributed as significantly to ethnic consciousness formation as the common cultural characteristics brought over from the old country. Theories dealing with formation of racial consciousness among racial minorities support this assertion. Robert Blauner (1969), who formulated the influential internal colony model, states that ethnic consciousness stems from the colonized position to which nonwhites were relegated, making them aware of their differences (Cited in Griswold del Castillo, 1979, pp. 103-105). In a book called *Conflict Sociology*, Randall Collins (1975) maintains that exclusion from the political and economic system, and differences in skin color, result in a growing self-awareness (Cited in Griswold del Castillo, 1979, pp. 103-105). The formation of ethnic consciousness among Mexican immigrants parallels the process, described earlier in this paper, experienced by Southwest Mexicans during the 19th century. In the early immigrant era, intense interethnic rivalry, police brutality, segregation, abuse in the workplace, and general rejection from the mainstream community served as the primary impetus for cohesion. For the immigrant, the pain from these violations was not alleviated by initial adaptive postures such as mutual aid, religiosity, cultural reinforcement, or the notion that soon they would be back in Mexico. Mexicans also mobilized community resources for the purposes of self-defense, but only after an immigrant nationalism pervaded, and cut across regional and class divisions within the *colonias*. Paul Taylor (1930) interviewed an immigrant in Texas who revealed the psychological mechanics of how nationalism was acquired in the United States. "The more wrong you [Anglos] say about Mexico the more I love it [Mexico]" (p. 272).

But more important for the argument presented here is that upper class status and behavior did not protect Mexicans from Anglo prejudice. Early in the history of the *colonias* Mexican immigrants, who back in Mexico were elevated above the common people, assumed that if they projected a positive Mexican image which they themselves held in high esteem, that Anglos would distinguish them from poorer and less educated Mexicans. When put to the test such optimism proved unwarranted. In Houston, for example, immigrant merchants and professionals, who founded *México Bello*, promoted Mexican high culture and prided themselves on their correct Mexican behavior. Isidro Ortiz (1979), one of the original members, indicated that *México Bello* "would promote the Mexican culture and heritage...in the United States to remove any stigma of shame at being Mexican...." But when the group sought to hold their elegant Black and White social at the Rice Hotel Ballroom they were turned away in humiliation (Rosales, 1981, p. 235).

Then in 1929, *La Orquesta Típica de Magnolia*, a highly polished musical ensemble which interpreted and performed folkloric as well as classical pieces, was formed. The group became the pride of the *colonia* and complimented the efforts to promote a positive image that Anglos could respect and even admire. The group did receive favorable publicity in the English language newspapers but bitter disappointment resulted when the orchestra was denied lodgings in Galveston while it was on tour (Rosales, 1985, p. 235). A similar attitude was shared in other Mexican immigrant communities by the immigrant elites. For example, *El Amigo del Hogar*, in 1927, advocated boycotting the Garden Theater in East Chicago when Mexicans were forced to sit in the balcony because "we should be treated like the white race as they do in other theaters" (*El Amigo del Hogar* July 17, 1927).

Since Anglos did not readily recognize the differences that back in Mexico distinguished "la gente decente" from "la gente baja," and rejected all Mexicans on racial and cultural grounds, middle class immigrants found this constant discrimination humiliating and made common cause with their working class compatriots. They were able then to appeal to their more provincial compatriots by manipulating cultural symbols with which they were intimately familiar.

José Anguiano (1974), a peasant immigrant who was almost illiterate when he arrived in East Chicago during the 1920s, said in an interview:

> When I first arrived here I was a greenhorn, I barely had learned to tie shoe laces [an ironic reference to his having only worn sandals in Mexico]. But I would observe the more educated members of the *colonia* and attempt to emulate their speech, their mannerisms, and I discovered that I was abysmally ignorant about the history of my country (Translation by Author).

Another reason why immigrant businessmen professionals, entertainers, artists and leaders of the Mexican organizations would pursue ethnic cohesiveness was because of their dependence, in the extremely segregated Mexican *colonias*, on exclusively Mexican clientele. Economically they had nothing to gain and everything to lose if ethnic cohesiveness would dissipate because of assimilation or acceptance of Mexicans by the Anglo community.

The *México lindo* source of identity, however virulent it seemed in the initial *colonia* building stage, did not survive the massive repatriation of Mexicans provoked by the Great Depression. It was apparent to those remaining in the United States that another strategy was needed in order to break down the obstacles to social and economic mobility. Americanization was seized upon by the new leadership through organizations such as the League of United Latin American Citizens (LULAC). Besides, the leaders were no longer immigrants who intended to return to Mexico.

These leaders consisted of a new and younger generation who either were born in the United States or were very young upon arrival. They could not identify with the symbolism perpetuated in previous decades by immigrant leaders, and so they pursued an assimilationist identity. This identity was forged by a embracing an Americanized view of themselves with a truncated and watered down version of the "Mexico Lindo" vision. For example, *Fiestas Patrias* continued to be celebrated and homages continued to be paid to the culture of Mexico, but by a definitely Americanizing generation. The symbols of the "Lost Land" concept, such as ties to the land and intimacy with the environment, continued to have relevance, but mainly in the regions settled by Hispanics in the old Southwest.

References

Blauner, R. (1969). Internal colonization and ghetto revolt. Social Problems, 16, 393-408.
Bodnar, J. (1973). The formation of ethnic consciousness: Slavic immigrants in Steeltown. In J. Bodnar (Ed.), The ethnic experience in Pennsylvania (pp. 309-330). Lewisburg, Pennsylvania: Bucknell University.
Brading, D. A. (1973). "Creole nationalism and Mexican liberalism," Journal of Inter American Studies, 15, 139-190.
Chávez, J. R. (1984). The lost land: The Chicano image of the Southwest. Albuquerque: University of New Mexico.
Collins, R. (1975). Conflict sociology: Towards an explanatory science. New York: Academic Press.
García, M. T. (1981). Desert immigrants: The Mexicans of El Paso. New Haven: Yale University.
González, L. (1972). San Jose de Gracia: Mexican town in transition. Austin: University of Texas Press.
Griswold del Castillo, R. (1979). The Los Angeles barrio, 1850-1890: A social history. Berkeley: University of California.
Johnson, J. J. (1965). The new Latin American nationalism. Yale Review (Winter), 187-204.
Jones, M. A. (1960). American immigration. Chicago: University of Chicago.
Mirandé, A. (1987). Gringo justice. South Bend: University of Notre Dame.
Olson, J. S. (1979). The ethnic dimension in American history. New York: St. Martin's.
Rosales, F. A. (1976). The regional origins of Mexicano immigrants to Chicago during the 1920s. Aztlan, 7, 187-201.
Rosales, F. A. (1985). Mexicans in Houston: The struggle to survive. The Houston Review, 3, 224-247.
Rosenbaum, R. J. (1981). Mexicano resistance in the Southwest: The sacred right of self-preservation. Austin: University of Texas.
Schmidt, H. C. (1978). The roots of lo Mexicanismo: Self and society in Mexican thought. College Station: Texas A&M.
Sinkin, R. N. (1979). The Mexican reform, 1855-1876: A study in liberal nation building. Austin: University of Texas.
Smith, T. L. (1978). Religion and ethnicity in America. The American Historical Review, 83, 1155-1185.
Sociedad Benito Juárez (May 5, 1919). *Acta Primordial de la Sociedad Benito Juárez.* Houston: Typscript in Houston Metropolitan Research Center (HMRC).

Taylor, P. S. (1929). Mexican labor in the United States: Valley of the South Platte, Colorado. Berkeley: University of California.
Taylor, P. S. (1930). Mexican labor in the United States: Dimmit County, Winter Garden District. Berkeley: University of California.
Taylor, P. S. (1932). Mexican labor in the United States: Chicago and the Calumet region. Berkeley: University of California.
Taylor, P. S. (1933). A Spanish-Mexican community: Arandas in Jalisco, Mexico. Berkeley: University of California.
Turner, F. (1968). The dynamic of Mexican nationalism. Chapel Hill: University of North Carolina.

Interviews

Anguiano, J., East Chicago, Indiana , 1974.
Hernandez, H., Miller, Indiana, 1974.
Ortiz, I. in *Houston Post*, January 21, 1979

Newspapers

El Amigo del Hogar, East Chicago, Indiana.
La Gaceta Mexicana, Houston, Texas.

Mexican American Identity

Chapter III

Bernal and Martinelli

Expressive Ethnicity and Ethnic Identity in Mexico and Mexican America

by

John L. Aguilar
Arizona State University

This chapter takes a multicultural look at the effects of the expressive aspects of ethnicity (particularly in the form of ethnic movements) for self-perception and collective identity among ethnic minorities, particularly Mexican Americans. It argues that recognition by specialists and the public at large of the psychological importance of expressive ethnicity has been virtually eclipsed in social research by an emphasis on the instrumental side of ethnicity which refers to actions directed toward material (political or economic) goals. Expressive ethnicity is also goal oriented, but here the end is realized in the behavior itself. It is symbolic action that is inherently gratifying and performed essentially for this gratification. Discussion of the importance of the expressive functions of ethnicity and ethnic movements will proceed against the background of two additional dichotomies: majority group ethnicity and minority group ethnicity, on the one hand, and collateral and stratified ethnicity, on the other.

In the Chiapas highlands of southeastern Mexico, Indian communities mark themselves off from one another by means of costumes, religious practices, linguistic variations and other emblems of distinctiveness. This form of ethnicity, occurring in terms of groups that are unranked (i.e., horizontally situated) vis-a-vis one another, is termed here collateral ethnicity. At the same time, Ladinos (as non-Indian Mexicans are called in this region) consider themselves to be superior to all Indians. This attitude (or claim) occurs in the context of what is termed here stratified ethnicity, a salient aspect of the region's class system in which Indians are socially and politically subordinate to Ladinos. This chapter focuses on stratified ethnicity, the form experienced by Mexican Americans, and distinctions between majority group ethnicity and minority group ethnicity. In this context ethnicity represents political "strife between ethnic groups in the course of which people stress their identity and exclusiveness" (Cohen, 1969, p. 4). This stress on identity includes a rebellious declaration by the members of a minority group of their positive collective worth. And, of course, such efforts to enhance the status of one's group (if not in the eyes of the dominant society, at least one's own) is one means of enhancing one's self-image as well. Thus, with stratified ethnicity, the expressive dimension also pertains to psychological and ideological adaptations, mainly in terms of the minority individual's sense of his group's worth.

Ethnic Identity as Resource

It is widely agreed that "ethnic identity is a resource that individuals and groups use to structure transactions with others" (Foster & White, 1982, p. 122). Most often this principle points to occasions where individuals and groups claim for themselves the rights attached to particular identities in pursuit of goals. For example, a Chiapas Ladino, in defending the existing ethnic division of labor as eternal (Nash, 1972, considers this to be a major function of the Ladinos' racial ideology) explained to this author that Indians are born to "work in the sun" (i.e., in agricultural and other forms of unskilled labor), while Ladinos are born to "work in the shade" (i.e., in various forms of skilled or at least non-manual work). As this example illustrates, groups not only legitimize their advantages in terms of ethnic identity claims for themselves but also pursue their goals in terms of identities assigned to others. This is the collective counterpart of the "altercasting" interactional device (Weinstein & Deutschberger, 1963) in which an individual attempts to achieve goals by creating a role for another that supports those goals. Such roles are sometimes defined in terms of imputed genetic inequalities. Mexican American racial stereotypes have served to rationalize economic abuses in the American Southwest--witness the former California senator George Murphy's claim that "Mexicans are ideal for 'stoop' labor--after all, they are built close to the ground" (Feagin, 1978, p. 296). Judith Friedlander's

(1975) study of ethnicity in Hueyapan reveals a pattern of interethnic altercasting, and is appropriately subtitled, "A Study of <u>Forced</u> Identity in Contemporary Mexico" (italics added).

In the history of highland Chiapas the altercasting tactic has been a major part of the Spaniards' and later the Ladinos' efforts to control the region's Indian population. Ever since the Spanish Conquest, Indians have been defined as inferior by Ladinos. This "inferiority" has identified a population of people obliged to be subservient to Ladinos and who may be exploited by the latter with a degree of moral impunity. Today it is a commonplace for Ladinos to cheat and abuse Indians as a routine feature of interethnic relations, and the basis for this impunity is the racial inferiority imputed by Ladinos to Indians (Aguilar, 1979). This is a clear example of majority group ethnicity.

Some anthropologists such as Tax (1942), Stavenhagen (1970), Vogt (1969), Colby and sociologist van den Berghe (1961) would disagree, maintaining instead that cultural rather than racial differences divide the populations of the Chiapas and Guatemalan highlands. Their argument rests on the absence of distinct races in these areas. Yet research in Chiapas (Aguilar, 1979, 1982) and Guatemala (Brintnall, 1979) shows that the presence or absence of actual racial variations is irrelevant. What is relevant is the operation of "social race" (Wagley, 1968, p. 156): racial imputations made by one group to another. While it is true that Ladinos most frequently define the region's ethnic groups in terms of cultural variations, they also explain these variations with reference to imputed biological inequalities.

Ethnicity in this sense refers not only to the act of defining boundaries between groups but also the act of ranking those groups. The groups involved in this processes are politically and economically unequal majority groups and minority groups (Vincent, 1974). In this sense, Chiapas' Indians are--despite their numerical majority--ethnic minorities, and their ethnic identity is defined in contrast to that of the Ladino. Between the various Indian communities of the area (Huistan, Tenejapa, Chamula, Zinacantan, etc.) there is, of course, a sense of mutual exclusiveness, the "we-they" sentiments characteristic of ethnic phenomena. Between Indians and Ladinos, however, the separation is defined also, and perhaps primarily, in terms of superiority-inferiority and dominance-subservience relations. Because of its great number of Indian groups, the highland region of Chiapas has been described, ethnically, as a multiple society, but with respect to majority and minority group relations it is clearly a dual society. And it represents, since the time of the Spanish Conquest, an engineered duality resting on ideological racism (cf. Aguirre-Beltran, 1979).

Ethnic Movements

Such situations, wherein negative racial identities (and their corresponding disparaged social positions) are assigned by a majority group to a minority group, form an important basis of ethnic movements. Ethnic movements are defined here as large scale social rebellions involving the creation or reinterpretation of ethnic symbols. They are to be distinguished from ethnic campaigns, smaller scale efforts on the part of some members of an ethnic group to mobilize around existing ethnic symbols for competition in particular interethnic contests. Ethnic movements are often responses to the oppressions of majority group ethnicity. The responses themselves are examples of minority group ethnicity, attempts to adjust symbolically and behaviorally to the chronic denigration of assigned negative identities.

Such rebellions characteristically involve ideological counter-statements which upgrade the view a group has of itself. Such a counter-statement is seen in the Black American theme of the 1960s: "Black is Beautiful." A synonym for the Civil Rights Movement (i.e., the struggle for equitable access to rights and resources) was the "Black Liberation Movement" (liberation from both political-economic and psychological oppression). Among Mexican American youth, the label Chicano was adopted specifically in opposition to the term Mexican American because the latter was, in their perception at least, the label assigned them by Anglo Americans. This act of self-identification expressed a general aspiration for self-determination, including a repudiation of the stereotype of Mexican Americans as incapable of self-government. The slogans Brown Power and Black Power also denoted both instrumental (political and economic) and expressive (psychological) goals. This is not to say, however, that all minority individuals needed to upgrade their view of themselves, or that they saw themselves through the eyes of the white majority, but many did, particularly among the poor classes within minority groups.

Expressive and Instrumental Ethnicity

As stated above, most contemporary research on ethnicity and ethnic movements has an instrumentalist focus. Abner Cohen (1969) has argued, for example, that "Hausa [ethnic] identity and Hausa exclusiveness in Ibadan [West Africa] are the expressions not so much of strong "tribalistic" sentiment as vested economic interests" (p. 14). In this conception, the ethnic group is no more than an informal interest group. And for decades researchers have arrived at similar conclusions in their approach to ethnicity as response to the demands of resource competition. Such an approach is undoubtedly useful. Clearly the instrumental functions of ethnicity are often part of its raison d'etre. As long as ethnic minorities are deprived of political and economic power, ethnic movements will have instrumental aims. But it is also the case that as long as such minorities are also deprived of self-determinations and social dignity, such movements will also serve expressive functions. Expressive ethnicity has received some attention, of course, in psychological discussions of the causes and effects of intergroup prejudice, but its significance has been most appreciated by the more radical critics of colonialism, such as Franz Fanon (1968), Albert Memmi (1965) and, for "internal" colonialism in the United States, Malcom X (Breitman, 1965).

In addition to the use of symbolic resources for their value in mobilizing groups for political and economic competition, the value of symbolic resources also derives from their expressive significance. In such cases ethnicity claims are made not only for the utilitarian ends they may facilitate but as ends in themselves--that is to say, because it simply feels good to make them. This applies to both minority and majority groups: Mexican Americans enjoy asserting their ethnic virtues, while many of the poorest Anglo Americans delight in the conviction that they are at least superior to ethnic minorities. The delights provided by victories in the current "English Only" movement serve as examples of the expressive (and possibly instrumental) functions in the context of majority group ethnicity.

The analysis of majority-minority group relations must acknowledge the reality of both class structures and class conflict, on the one hand, and status groups and status competition, on the other. As Joseph Hraba (1979) reminds us, ". . . systems of racial stratification not only serve in the protection of wealth and power, they also help a wealthy and powerful group in the conservation of its honor... Intergroup conflict and racial stratification involve the issue of honor as much as they do the distribution of wealth and power" (p. 106). And we should add that one group's honor sometimes entails another group's dishonor. In the Chiapas highlands, for example, Ladinos employ the psychological maneuver of dumping the negative qualities--e.g., the "backwardness"-- they would deny for themselves (but which they know metropolitan Mexicans impute to them) onto their Indian neighbors. Indeed, throughout Mexico's colonial period many Spanish colonists claimed for themselves the rank denied them in Spain in contrast to Blacks and Indians, the New World equivalents of Old World Muslims and Jews. Today, Ladinos continue to proclaim their *limpieza de sangre*, their freedom from the taint of Indian blood. For this reason, and for purposes of economic exploitation, Ladinos need the social category of Indian (*Indio*). A far less extreme, but parallel, situation can be observed among Mexican Americans. Although it is usually denied, within Mexican American society some individuals define their class hierarchy in part on the basis of color, reflecting their own rejection of Indian "blood."

For minority groups, ethnic movements are similar to the identity or status politics occurring today among American Gays and Lesbians. They are similar both in terms of their instrumental goals--nondiscrimination in the market place (jobs and housing)--and in their expressive aspects.

For minorities, at least, ethnic ideological movements provide a psychological defense (at least they provide a symbolic resource to be used) against racism's chronic erosion of their self-esteem. It is inherently gratifying to collectively affirm their worth and to repudiate the majority group's "social definitions which rationalize their deprivations of freedom and autonomy" (Kuper, 1974, p. 109).

Ethnic Awareness and Ethnic Consciousness

In the context of stratified ethnicity, then, identity claims serve not only to contrast "us" and "them," but also to assert the worth of one's self and group. After all, there is most likely to exist within the minority group a perception of its distinctiveness vis-a-vis the majority group before the rise of an ethnic movement, before the minority has awakened to its interests, rights, and worth. What the ethnic movement generates is not so much an ethnic awareness, a sense of the group's boundaries, as it does an ethnic consciousness, a sense of its collective interests, rights, and worth. This distinction, taken from McKay and Lewins (1978), parallels the difference between the ethnic category (in terms of a group's cultural, physical and other traits) and an ethnic group (in terms of its sense of its common interests). In the development of ethnic consciousness the negative values placed by others on their identity and way of life are now replaced by positive values which, it must be repeated, is a state that feels good. It is "egosyntonic," a psychological state in which the individual's ego and superego are in agreement. Such a state can be an end in itself. Minority group ethnicity thus often has a psychological significance too often ignored in studies of ethnicity.

Mexican American Identity

With regard to the instrumentalist orientation, McKay and Lewins (1978) remark that while they have "no reservations about applying [the] 'theory of political and economic mobilization'. . . to some ethnic groups in certain situations, [they] feel that it does not apply to all ethnic phenomena. They contend, further, that sometimes ethnic phenomena are best understood in terms of "strategies to solve problems of identity, belief, and culture and perhaps only secondarily in terms of political strategies. . . . . In other contexts conflict and competition arise which are based not on material resources but on ideological differences" (p. 422). It would seem obvious that ethnic communities sometimes define or emphasize ethnic boundaries in order to mobilize themselves or stress their status as moral communities (or political teams) and that the resulting sense of cohesiveness is a resource in situations of competition with other groups for material resources. It seems equally obvious, however, that members of ethnic communities like to emphasize their internal commodities (and perhaps to exaggerate their distinctiveness) in order to foster a sense of community, a sense of 'we-ness' as an expressive end in itself.

Clearly it would be more instructive to examine ways in which instrumental and expressive aspects of ethnicity interact rather than to generalize about the relative importance of one over the other. Undoubtedly, the relative importance of each will vary with situations. And it is likely that most situations involve admixtures of instrumental and expressive functions.

Sometimes the instrumental functions of ethnicity may be served without this being intended by actors themselves. Paradoxically, this is sometimes missed when research fails to understand behavior in terms of its meaning for the actors. Instrumentally-oriented research often identifies associations between patterns of observable behavior and their overt political-economic consequences, and then infers the consequences to be the intended goals of the observed behavior. In many cases the inference is correct. At other times ethnicity, when examined from the actor's perspective, may be seen to consist of rebellious expressive reactions to the racism of majority group ethnicity, and the instrumental gains may be the unintended results of such reactions. One rather obvious example of how this may happen: when people feel good about themselves due to their group membership, a consequence is heightened intragroup cohesiveness which, as social psychological studies of group performance reveal, promotes group effectiveness through enhanced cooperation. Thus, the expressive actions of ethnicity may serve instrumental ends, but only as the latent functions of such actions.

Movement Leaders

The efficacy of ethnicity for competition for economic and political resources explains the failure of both the liberal expectation that racial and ethnic discrimination would eventually disappear and the radical expectations that ethnic attachments would be displaced along class lines (cf. Gordon, 1975). It should be noted, however, that the instrumental goals of an ethnic group can be achieved only after the group has been mobilized. This mobilization is problematical; it doesn't just happen. It requires, as Vincent (1974) notes, the active instigation of individuals and organizations. Following Rabushka and Shepsele (1972), Ronald Cohen (1978) adds that "the quality and content of leadership is crucial at this point. Leaders. . . . enhance their own positions. . . . by defining conflicts, raising hopes, and articulating and explaining fears and frustrations. . . .In so doing they. . . .try to unify ethnic-based support for . . . issues behind themselves as leaders" (p. 396). This usually applies to ethnic goals after an ethnic movement/rebellion has occurred or is underway. But these larger rebellions also require leaders--their Martin Luther Kings, Malcom Xs, Corky Gonzalezes and Reies Tijerinas.

It may well be that the best way for such leaders to mobilize their ethnic fellows in ethnic campaigns is to address their expressive needs. This will probably involve harnessing the emotional energy attached to group symbols of ethnic pride. If leaders are cynically utilitarian in their role in ethnic campaigns, it is almost certainly the case that followers participate mainly for the satisfaction of expressive goals. Indeed, entrepreneurial efforts to mobilize the participation of individuals in ethnic campaigns are less likely to succeed when based solely on promises of material gain. This is particularly so where, as in most instances, the perceived and actual chances of such gains are very slim. People are more likely to be galvanized into political and economic action after the emergence of a favorable ideological climate. Such a climate is the result of an ethnic movement which is born of a minority group's awareness of the more solid prospect of introducing to their lives a quality of rebellion, a posture of defiance. Such an expressive rebellion is in fact revolutionary; it entails a radical change in the style, if not the structure, of intergroup relations, and in the nature of the minority individual's self-concept. Without this identity dimension, the participation of minorities in ethnic competition may lack the intensity, the energizing chauvinism seen in successful ethnic campaigns.

Economic Independence: Examples from Central America

While majority group ethnicity, particularly as expressed in racism, forms an important basis of ethnic movements, the causal connection is not a simple one, for sometimes majority group ethnicity does not result in minority group rebellions. A casual comparison of two communities, Teopisca (Chiapas), and San Pedro (Guatemala), suggests the importance of economic independence as a determining factor in the emergence of ethnic movements. In Teopisca, Indians have for generations experienced the most intense economic exploitation and social denigration, yet they show no signs of minority group ethnicity. Indeed, when the members of an Indian barrio sought advice from a government official on how to petition the government for materials for the construction of a school house, they were advised to send with their request a photograph of themselves dressed in Indian costumes (home-made collarless shirts, knee-length pants and sandals--or shoeless). A resident of that *barrio* reported that he and his neighbors decided not to "demean" themselves in that way. Here we see both a sense of shame (cf. Aguilar, 1982) regarding their Indian identity and a refusal even to claim identity for instrumental purposes. In addition, Teopiscan Indians dare not publicly define themselves in opposition to the negative identity assigned them by Ladinos, either by claiming Ladino status for themselves or by redefining their Indian identity in positive terms. For the most part this reflects their economic dependence on Ladinos. In opposing Ladino definitions one runs the risk of being labeled <u>alzado</u> (rebellious) and subjected to economic intimidation with respect to employment and patronage.

The town of San Pedro provides a contrasting picture. Waldemar Smith (1975) describes how Pedranos not only accepted their Indian identity, but claimed it as a virtue. This followed a process of economic mobility which resulted in the Indians of San Pedro enjoying a higher economic position than that of their Ladino neighbors in the neighboring town of San Marcos.

With their economic development, Indians of San Pedro "modernized" their lifestyle, adopting the use of western medicine, electricity, running water and appliances, as well as higher education. This was not an attempt, however, to Ladinoize themselves. At the same time that they adopted these conveniences they insisted on their distinctive Indian identity. In Teopisca the rare Indian who achieves economic independence tries to "pass" into the Ladino category. To accomplish this he must move to a location where his origins are unknown, a reflection of the importance of race and descent in this stratification system.

Indians of San Pedro did not use ethnicity in their efforts to achieve economic mobility. Rather, according to Smith (1975), this mobility resulted primarily from a set of favorable objective economic circumstances: educational opportunities, good flat valley land, central location, tailoring skills, high demand for their weaving skills in Guatemala City, and an effective system of capitalist middlemen to market their products. Their ethnic movement occurred against a background of economic abundance rather than deprivation; they asserted their ethnic pride after their achievement of economic independence. It was, in fact, the wealthier Pedranos who led their ethnic movement. It should also be noted that ethnic movements in the United States have been initiated and maintained mainly by middle class and mobile minorities, particularly college students. The ethnic movement at San Pedro is clearly to be understood as a social and psychological end in itself rather than as a means for organizing people for economic gains. It was not an instrumental reaction to economic exploitation; it was an expressive movement against social denigration.

The Bottom Line

Given the foregoing discussion, it can be seen that it would be narrow-sighted to view ethnic rebellions only in negative terms, i.e., merely as pathological indications of "social disorganization." The ethnic movements of the 1960s may have had little effect in meeting the material needs of most American minorities, but the expressive functions of such movements have clearly contributed to the minority individual's psychological adjustment and success in life.

References

Aguilar, J. L. (1979). Class and ethnicity as ideology: Stratification in a Mexican town. Ethnic Groups: An International Periodical of Ethnic Studies, 2, 109-131.

Aguilar, J. L. (1982). Shame, ethnicity, and ethnic relations: A psychological "process of domination" in southern Mexico. The Journal of Psychoanalytic Anthropology, 5, 155-171.

Aguirre-Beltrán, G. (1979). Regions of refuge (Monograph Number 12). Washington, DC: The Society for Applied Anthropology.

Breitman, G. (Ed.). (1965). Malcom X speaks. New York: Merit Publishers.

Brintnall, D. E. (1979). Race relations in the southeastern highlands of Mesoamerica. American Ethnologist, 6, 638-652.

Cohen, A. (1969). Custom and politics in urban Africa. Berkeley: University of California Press.

Cohen, R. (1978). Ethnicity: Problems and focus in anthropology. Annual Review of Anthropology, 7, 379-403.

Colby, R. & van den Berghe, P. (1961). Ethnic relations in southeastern Mexico. American Anthropologist, 63, 772-792.

Fanon, F. (1968). The wretched of the earth. New York: The Grove Press.

Feagin, J. (1978). Racial and ethnic relations. Englewood Cliffs, NJ: Prentice-Hall.

Foster, B. & White, G. M. (1982). Ethnic identity and perceived distance between ethnic categories. Human Organization, 41, 121-130.

Friedlander, J. (1975). Being Indian in Hueyapan: A study in forced identity in contemporary Mexico. New York: St. Martin's Press.

Gordon, M. (1975). Toward a general theory of racial and ethnic group relations. In D. Moynihan & N. Glazer (Eds.), Ethnicity: Theory and experience (pp. 84-110). Cambridge, MA: Harvard University Press.

Hraba, J. (1979). American ethnicity. Itasca, IL: F. E. Peacock Publishers, Inc.

Kuper, L. (1974). Race, class and power. Chicago: Aldine Publishing Company.

McKay, J. & Lewins, F. (1978). Ethnicity and the ethnic group: A conceptual analysis and reformulation. Ethnic and Racial Studies, 1, 412-427.

Memmi, A. (1965). The colonizer and the colonized. Boston: Beacon Press.

Nash, M. (1972). Race and the ideology of race. In P. Baxter & B. Sansom (Eds.), Race and social difference (pp. 111-122). Baltimore: Penguin Books.

Rabushka, A. & Shepsle, K. A. (1972). Politics in plural societies: A theory of democratic instability. Columbus, OH: Merrill.

Smith, W. (1975). Beyond the plural society: Economics and ethnicity in Middle American towns. Ethnology, 14, 225-243.

Stavenhagen, R. (1970). Classes, colonialism and acculturation. In I. L. Horowitz (Ed.), Masses in Latin America (pp. 235-289). New York: Oxford University Press.

Tax, S. (1942). Ethnic relations in Guatemala. America Indigena, 2 43-47.

Vincent, J. (1974). The structuring of ethnicity. Human Organization, 33, 375-379.

Vogt, E. Z. (1969). Zinacantan: A Mayan community in the highlands of Chiapas. Cambridge, MA: Belknap Press.

Wagley, C. (1968). The Latin American tradition. New York: Columbia University Press.

Weinstein, E. & Deutschberger, P. (1963). Some dimensions of altercasting. *Sociometry*, 26, 454-466.

Mexican American Identity

Section II

Mexican American Identity

Section II

Children and Youths

The growing multicultural population of the U. S. increases the importance of research on the ethnic identity of children and youths, in whom it emerges, forms, and establishes itself. The ethnic identity of adults has to differ in significant ways from that of children and adolescents. Before a certain age, children's understanding of who they are as ethnic individuals, and of their ethnic group membership, is likely to be limited both by their cognitive capacities as well as by the manner and degree to which their families transmit their culture to them. As children grow into adolescence, they face the formulation and incorporation of many identities into their self-concepts. These formulations are intimately related to the appraisals and feedback provided by the dominant society regarding their social identities. Some of this feedback may cause conflict and intrapersonal as well as interpersonal stress. Ethnic identity is but one of many identities with which adolescents must grapple and which they must resolve. The next two chapters provide some insights into the ethnic identity of young children and high school youths.

Emergence of Ethnic Identity

Martha Bernal and her associates present a theory about ethnic identity and its development in young children. Ethnic identity is viewed as a part of children's evolving self-concept, influenced by their enculturative experiences in their own culture and their acculturative experiences with the dominant society. In young children, ethnic identity is believed to have five components, e.g., ethnic self-identification and ethnic knowledge, and the content of these components is constrained by their cognitive maturation as well as their socialization.

An important part of Bernal et al's contribution is their effort to generate an instrument that can be used to measure ethnic identity in children of this age. They assess the children's understanding of their ethnic selves, and find that preschool Mexican American children have a basic and concrete, but rather limited, view of their ethnic identity. Children who speak Spanish are more likely to have better information about their ethnic identity than children who are monolingual English speaking. While their parents may teach them about their culture and ethnic traditions, preschool children simply may not be old enough to have the cognitive ability to process and understand aspects of their ethnic identity.

Assessment of Ethnic Identity by the Role/Identity Procedure

In his chapter dealing with Mexican American high school students, whose maturation and experience permits a much more complex sense of ethnic identity than that of preschool children, Kurt Organista is concerned with the measurement of the ethnic identity construct in a manner that addresses this complexity, and with assessment of the relationship between ethnic identity and psychological adjustment.

He adapts role/identity measurement used to assess gender role/identity to the study of ethnic identity. The procedure is based on the theory that ethnic identity is one of the multiple definitions or meanings of the self that are embodied in the individual's self-concept. These self-definitions or identities vary in their importance, both in their salience to the self-concept and in their influence in the individual's life experience. In ethnic individuals, ethnic identity is viewed as one of the most central and powerful identities. Identities are associated with particular interactional settings or roles; thus, the term role/identity, with identity referring to the internal component of self and role to the external component. Organista departs from the conventional role/identity methodology in applying role/identity theory to the study of adolescent ethnic identity. He finds that Mexican American and Anglo American adolescents have different conceptions of how Mexican, Anglo, and Black American high school students differ, but that these different conceptions are not related to psychological adjustment. In the end, he discusses possible methodological refinements.

Mexican American Identity

Chapter 4: The young Mexican American child's understanding of ethnic identity. M. E. Bernal, G. P. Knight, K. C. Organista, C. A. Garza, & B. M. Maez.

Chapter 5: Use of the role/identity procedure for measuring ethnic identity in Mexican American adolescents. K. C. Organista

Mexican American Identity

Chapter IV

The Young Mexican American Child's Understanding of Ethnic Identity

by

Martha E. Bernal, George P. Knight, Kurt C. Organista, Camille A. Garza, and Berlie M. Maez
Arizona State University

In 1980, the United States Census Bureau made the decision to stop identifying Hispanics by Spanish surname, and instead to permit Hispanics to self-identify. One major social policy implication of this decision is that the official numbers of Hispanics, and consequently their access to national resources, depends upon self-identification. How that Hispanic self-identification is established and maintained is a question that is central to the continuing growth of the Hispanic American population, and to their political and economic status.

Social scientists strongly suspect that parents are influential as transmitters of ethnic culture, although this influence has only recently received critical empirical exploration (e.g., Knight, Bernal, Garza, Cota, & Ocampo, 1991). In this decade, Hispanics need to begin to concentrate their collective energies on understanding the factors that maintain Hispanic self-identification in children and youth. In order to promote that understanding, it is necessary to generate a theoretical framework for how ethnic identity emerges and develops in children. Furthermore, specification and measurement of ethnic identity is vital, since without the means to measure it reliably and validly there can be no scientific progress. This paper addresses the issues of conceptualization and measurement of ethnic identity in Mexican American children, and explores the question of cultural transmission from parents to children.

This chapter first describes a theoretical framework for understanding the development of ethnic identity in ethnic minority children. Then two research studies that explore the emergence of ethnic identity in preschool Mexican American children are presented. A questionnaire constructed for the study of ethnic identity in young children was used, and results are reported for different components of ethnic identity. In addition, relationships between the children's use of Spanish and parental cultural characteristics, and their ethnic identity were explored.

Theoretical Framework

Definition of ethnic identity in children. Ethnic identity refers to children's (1) perception that they possesses characteristics and practice customs of their ethnic group, (2) feelings about membership in their ethnic group, and (3) their knowledge of their ethnic group, since they need this knowledge in order to identify themselves as group members. When children manifest these perceptions, knowledge, preferences, feelings, customs, role behaviors, and values behaviorally, as in the use of language, preferences for own ethnic group companions, and ethnic self-labels, the multidimensional aspects of ethnic identity can be measured. Five components of ethnic identity will be measured: ethnic self-identification, ethnic constancy, knowledge of ethnic role behaviors, use of ethnic role behaviors, and feelings and preferences about own ethnic group membership.

Conceptual framework. Ethnic identity is regarded as part of the individual's answer to the question, "Who am I?" and is viewed as part of the self. According to Lewis and Brooks-Gunn (1979), the self is a cognitive inference which children progressively construct as they interact with the social environment. In turn the children's selves also change as this interaction with others continues. That is, children gather information about their selves from their social world and concurrently continue a process of building upon what they already know about their selves. As children gradually undergo this process, they learn self-descriptions and self-definitions, and they form a differentiation of themselves as distinct from others. This differentiation of self is intimately related to the surrounding social groups: the content of their self-descriptions takes form as children observe the evaluations of others about themselves and incorporate their judgements into their self-definitions.

For ethnic minority children, the social groups that provide these evaluations include their ethnic minority culture and the dominant culture (but other minority cultures also may be present). Their own ethnic group socializes or enculturates them as ethnic group members, and determines their ethnic identity. However, in the inevitable process of acculturation to the dominant culture, depending on the positive or negative nature of that process, children may experience comfort or discomfort with their ethnic identity. Such dominant culture evaluations may determine whether children value, retain, reject, or discard their ethnic identity. In other words, children's ethnic identity is molded and remolded as a joint product of ethnic group socialization experiences and interactions with the dominant culture. The investigation of children's ethnic identity must take into account at least two factors: (1) the kinds of adjustments minority children make to the attitudes and practices of the dominant culture toward ethnic minorities, and (2) the differing impact of these experiences and adjustments on their ethnic identity depending upon the developmental periods when they occur. At the age of 6 years, the recently immigrated Mexican child may quickly learn not to speak Spanish in front of school authorities, but continue to prefer use of Spanish and Mexican classmates in a multicultural low income school setting. At the age of 13 years, this same child attending a middle class largely white school may experience shame in his or her ethnic group membership and deny knowing Spanish or being Mexican.

The developmental model of ethnic identity used in this research is based on Harter's (1983) theoretical and empirical work on the "self-system," as well as on Fischer's (1980) adaptation of Piagetian theory and Selman's (1980) cognitive-developmental theory. Harter (1983) refers to the self-system as a central unifying set of related theories about the self that involve self-concept, self-esteem, etc., i.e., self-descriptions. Harter organizes the developing child's self-descriptions across cognitive structural levels and contents for different age levels, and identifies the nature of these developing self-descriptions for different domains of the self, such as the cognitive self, the social self, and the physical self.

In this chapter, the domain of ethnic identity has been added to the domains of the self already identified by Harter. By adapting Harter's model so it includes the ethnic self, it is possible to identify children's developmental changes in self-descriptions about ethnic identity. The pattern is shown in Table 1. Younger children aged 4-7 years use simple, concrete descriptions of physical atributes and appearance that are distinctive of ethnic/racial inheritances, such as "I'm brown." They use basic categories for ordering these descriptions, but these categories may have empty labels that do not have much meaning. For example, a child may refer to herself as "Mexican" and explain she is Mexican "Because I live in a Mexican house," or "Because my mommy told me so." Children also may engage in and describe ethnic behaviors such as " I speak Spanish" and food preferences such as "I eat frijoles" but may not associate these behaviors with their ethnic group.

Older 7-10 year old children, who are more mature cognitively, may be expected to improve their ethnic self-descriptions and categories by adding information to them. For example, "I'm Mexican because my parents come from Mexico." They understand that their ethnic characteristics are permanent or constant, "I was born Mexican and will be Mexican when I grow up." They know and engage in more ethnic behaviors, and identify them as ethnic, e.g., "I go to church to visit the Virgin of Guadalupe from Mexico." Two other kinds of self- descriptions may develop. They may begin to show emerging biculturality, "I can be Mexican in some places but not in others." They also begin to develop feelings about their ethnic group membership that manifest themselves as loyalty, preference, pride, or even shame. This chapter deals with younger children, and assesses self-descriptions for younger children only.

Research on Ethnic Identity of Preschool Children

Two studies were conducted that assessed the ethnic identity of Mexican American children aged 4 to 5 years. In Study 1, ethnic identity was related to language spoken by the children. In Study 2, the methodology of the first study was modified and a larger sample was used. Language again was related to ethnic identity, and in addition the relationship between the children's ethnic knowledge and their parents' ethnic background was evaluated.

Study 1

The subjects of the first study were 24 Mexican American children (12 boys and 12 girls) drawn from different multicultural Head Start classrooms in Denver, Colorado. Parent consent was obtained for all the children. The classrooms from which these children were drawn were selected so that at least half the children were Mexican American, and there were one or more Anglo as well as Black children in the classroom. To increase the likelihood that the children had heard others speaking the Spanish language, it was required that there be at least one Spanish-speaking child in the class. The children had been attending Head Start together for at least six months so they had the time and opportunity to become acquainted. Their mean age was 60 months (SD=8.3; range=48 to 78). Parental ratings of the children's ability to speak Spanish were used to identify 12 children who spoke Spanish, i.e., were either monolingual Spanish-speaking or bilingual in Spanish and English, and 12 children who were monolingual English-speaking.

An Ethnic Identity Questionnaire composed of a series of tasks and questions was devised to assess ethnic identity. This questionnaire was translated into Spanish, then back-translated into English to assure equivalence of meaning. It was administered in either English or Spanish, depending upon the child's preference. The experimenters were four Mexican American females who were bilingual.

Instructional Label Pretest. This pretest was administered to teach the task to the child. The experimenter said, "I am going to say some words. Tell me after I say each one whether the word is about you. Are you a _____?" Then nine different words (e.g., child, parent, boy, girl) were presented. After all the words were presented, the child was asked, "Which one of these words that is about you (words child used) is more like you than the others?

Ethnic Label. The Instructional Label Pretest procedure was repeated, using a set of 12 ethnic terms, including Hispanic, Spanish, Chicano, Mexican, and American, plus other ethnic labels. If the child identified as American, the experimenter said, "That's right, you're American, and what other word is also about you, more like you than any other word?"

Peer Naming. This task and the Ethnic and Racial Category task described below required the use of individual photographs of children in the class. Photographs of each child clad in a black "judge's robe" were taken under standard lighting conditions. The experimenter laid out the photos in front of the child and said, "These are photographs of the children who are in your class. Let's see how many children you can name." Then she picked up the child's own photo followed by each of the other photos and asked, "Who is this?" When all photos had been shown, the experimenter identified the children whom the child did not know.

Table 1

Predicted Self-Descriptions Concerning
Ethnic Identity in Mexican American Children
at Two Developmental Stages

Self-descriptions at ages 4-6 yrs.	Self-descriptions at ages 7-10
Simple, concrete descriptions of physical attributes and appearance to characterize their ethnic self. E.g., "I'm brown."	More psychological self-descriptions that are single abstractions.
May have basic categories for ordering ethnic self-description, e.g., "Mexican," but categories have "empty" labels that have little meaning. E.g., "I'm Mexican (because) I live in a Mexican house."	Categories have more meaning. "I'm Mexican because my parents come from Mexico."
Does not have ethnic constancy.	Understands ethnic constancy. "I was born Mexican and will be Mexican when I grow up."
Engages in and describes ethnic role behaviors and food preferences. "I eat frijoles." May not associate these behaviors with own group.	Knows and engages in more ethnic role behaviors and associates more behaviors with own group. "I go to church to visit the Virgin of Guadalupe from Mexico."

Instructional Ethnic and Racial Categories Pretest. Drawings of five four-footed animals and five assorted objects were presented individually on cards. The pile of cards was presented to the child who was told, "Here are pictures of some animals and things. I want you to put all the animals right here in this box and the ones that are not animals over there in the other box." The experimenter correctly sorted the first two cards, then the cards were handed to the child for sorting. Children who could not sort three of the four remaining animals correctly were excused from the study. After the child sorted all eight pictures, the experimenter asked three questions, "How do you know these are animals? How are the animals the same, how come they go together? How are the animals different from the other objects?"

Ethnic and Racial Categories. This task was used to assess the child's knowledge of ethnic (Spanish) and racial (Black and White) categories, and the cues used by the child to form the categories. The term, Spanish, was used because this was the term that parents used most often to refer to their ethnicity. If in the Ethnic Labels task the child indicated a preference for one of the other own-group ethnic labels (Chicano, Mexican, Hispanic), that term was used in assessing the child's own-group ethnic category. The procedure was the same as in the sorting of the animals, except that the children were asked to sort the photographs of the child's classmates, there was no sorting demonstration, and no children were eliminated from the study. First the child was asked to sort all the Black children into one box and non-Black children into the other, then the White children, and then the Spanish children. The photos were shuffled and mixed after the child completed sorting for each category. The three questions asked following each sorting completion used the words, Black, White, and Spanish (or other preferred label) instead of animals and things.

Ethnic Self-identification and Ethnic Constancy. Children who placed their own photograph in the Spanish box were told, "You put your picture in the box with the Spanish children. That means you are the same as the Spanish kids. How come you are Spanish? These questions were asked to determine the cues the children used in categorizing themselves into their own ethnic group. Then the children were asked, "Will you still be Spanish when you grow up?

Ethnic Information. The following questions were asked to further assess the children's knowledge of their ethnic group:

1. Is your family Spanish?   2. What is your last name?   3. Is your last name Spanish?

Knowledge of Ethnic Group Behaviors. The questions assessing children's knowledge of ethnic group behaviors required the child to identify which were own-ethnic group behaviors and which were not. Four nonsense set breaker questions were included to assess the child's attention. The child was told, "Now let's see what you know about Spanish children. There are things that only Spanish children do, and the other children don't do. Which of these are things that just the Spanish kids do?" Then each behavior was read to the child, prefaced by, "Do Spanish kids _____?" Some of the questions were: Eat frijoles or beans at home? Go to Mexico to visit their family? Have a pinata at their birthday party or at Christmas? Talk with their elbows? Pray to the Virgin of Guadalupe? Speak Spanish at home? Go to Italy to visit their family?

Use of Ethnic Role Behaviors. In order to assess whether the children engaged in any own-group ethnic role behaviors, even if they could not identify that the behavior were Spanish, the same knowledge of Ethnic Group Behaviors questions were administered again but the instructions were changed. The child was told, "I'm going to say some things that some kids do, and I want to find out if you do these things or not." Then the 18 questions were asked again, but prefaced by "Do you _____?"

To reduce testing time and redundancy effects, the Use of Ethnic Group Behaviors questions were administered a week after the knowledge of Ethnic Group Behaviors questions.

Study 2

Subjects for this study were 46 Mexican American children (22 girls and 24 boys) attending multicultural Head Start classrooms in Denver, Colorado, and their mothers. The children's mean age was 56 months (SD=6.8; Range 43-76). These children met the same criteria for participation as did those in Study 1. Parental ratings of their children's language use (1=speaks only English; 2=speaks mostly English; 3=speaks English and Spanish equally; 4=speaks mostly Spanish; 5=speaks only Spanish) indicated that 35 children were monolingual English speaking, and 11 were either bilingual or monolingual Spanish speaking. Ten of the children were first generation born in the U. S., four were 2nd generation, and 31 were third generation or more.

Mexican American Identity

The Ethnic Identity Questionnaire was modified based on numerous considerations. Only those sections of the Questionnaire that were changed from that used in Study 1 are noted below, with description of the changes. No new sections were added.

Ethnic and Racial Categories. Two changes were made in this task. To standardize the administration, a standard ethnic term was used with all children. The second change involved selection of terms for the categories so as to reduce confusion regarding their meaning. These terms used different concepts: race (Black, White), ethnicity (Anglo), ethnicity and nationality (Spanish, Mexican) or language (Spanish). Furthermore, although the term, Spanish, had been used because many Head Start families seemed to prefer this self-label, the data from the Study 1 suggested that the term implied to the children that only those who spoke Spanish were Spanish. The terms, Anglo and Mexican, were used in Study 2 because both referred to ethnic groups.

Knowledge of Ethnic Group Behaviors. Although 12 items were the same as in Study 1, the number of ethnic items was enlarged to 18, and only two set breakers were included in the list, for a total of 20 items. Because the previous version contained too many questions dealing with language spoken, the number of these items was reduced to three. Some behaviors dealing with other ethnic groups were added.

Use of Ethnic Group Behaviors. Changes in these items were those that were made for Knowledge of Ethnic Group Behaviors questions. No other changes were made.

Mothers of the children filled out Cuellar, Harris, and Jasso's (1980) Acculturation Rating Scale for Mexican Americans. This scale consists of 20 questions that cover language familiarity and usage, ethnic pride and identity, ethnic interaction, ethnic heritage, and generation in the U. S. The items are scored on a five-point Likert scale ranging from Mexican/Spanish to Anglo/English. It is available in both Spanish or English. Internal consistency and test-retest reliability are adequate, and the instrument has been used in a number of investigations (e.g., Montgomery & Orozco, 1984; Domino & Acosta, 1987). While the measure initially was validated on a sample of 239 psychiatric patients, hospital staff, and students (Cuellar, Harris, and Jasso, 1980), it has been cross-validated on a larger sample of 349 Mexican American and 101

Anglo American college students (Montgomery & Orozco, 1984).

The data analyses used in both studies were primarily designed to describe the children's ethnic knowledge and to assess any age differences in this knowledge. Most of the items from the interview were dichotomously scored to indicate knowledge of the concept assessed in the item. To save space, only the ethnic term, "Mexican" is used below, although in Study 1, the term "Spanish" was used by most of the children. The following rules were used to score the child's response as demonstrating some ethnic knowledge: (1) Correct Ethnic Self-Label - at least one correct ethnic self-label and no incorrect self-labels; (2) Correct Ethnic Sorting - putting the pictures of some Mexican, but no non-Mexican, children into the Mexican Box; (3) Correct Self Sorting - putting his/her own picture into the Mexican Box; (4) Reason for Self-sorting - having some meaningful reason for indicating that certain children belonged in the Mexican Box; (5) Ethnic Constancy - indicating that her/his family will remain Mexican; (6) Family Ethnic - indicating that her/his family is Mexican; (7) Name Ethnic - indicating that his/her last name is Mexican; (8) Knowledge of Ethnic Behaviors - correctly identifying some Mexican behaviors, and no non-Mexican behaviors, as Mexican; and (9) Use of Ethnic Behaviors - the number of Mexican Behaviors in which the child reported engaging. Further, those items included primarily as training items were also scored to indicate the child's knowledge of those concepts: (1) Gender Label - whether the child correctly identified his or her gender; and (2) Peer Naming - the percentage of the children in the class that the child could correctly identify. Children were dichotomized into those who were monolingual English speaking, i.e., spoke no Spanish, versus those who spoke both Spanish and English or were monolingual Spanish. The critical difference sought was whether or not they spoke any Spanish. While parental report of this nature cannot be considered an adequate measure of language proficiency, the relationship between how the children identified and their reported ability to speak Spanish was of interest.

The descriptive data from the items primarily used for training indicated that the children generally understood and were attentive to the interview. A majority of the children correctly identified their gender (66.7% and 91.3% in study 1 and 2, respectively), and could correctly name 75% or more of the children in their class (50.0% and 76.1%, respectively).

Column 1 of Table 2 presents the percentage for each study of the children who demonstrated some knowledge relating to each of the ethnic items. About a third of the children selected a correct ethnic self-label, and one-quarter to one-half of them correctly sorted their classmates into the Spanish or Mexican category. While about half of them correctly self-sorted into the Spanish or Mexican category, this performance was at chance level, since the children had a choice of putting their photographs in one of two piles. Similarly, since ethnic constancy required only a "yes-no" response, performance was at chance level. Children who gave reasons for self-sorting as Spanish or Mexican had reasons that were simple and referred to global physical or concrete characteristics, e.g., "I'm brown." It is clear from Table 2 that the children's knowledge concerning the ethnic concepts was very limited. There was a tendency for the children of Study 1 to have higher knowledge scores on most of the ethnic items that may have been due to the differences in the assessment procedures for the two studies. A percentage knowledge score for the component of Use of Ethnic Behaviors was not computed because this score refers to number of behaviors the child used, not to a criterion of correct response, as was the case for the other variables in Table 2.

In Study 1, half the children were able to correctly sort their classmates into Spanish and non-Spanish. This was not a very difficult task since half the subjects were Spanish-speaking. In Study 1 also, eight children who were Spanish-speaking gave as their reason for self-sorting as Spanish as some version of "I talk Spanish," but could not explain what talking Spanish meant. In Study 2, 11 or 24% of the children could group all their Mexican classmates correctly; these children could be said to have a concept of Mexican group membership. However, their concept of "Mexican" was an elementary one, since the reasons these children gave for the grouping were, "They have the same color," "Cause that's the Mexican box," "They look like Mexicans, the others don't," "Their mommas are Mexican." These descriptions of the Mexican group were global, concrete, and referred to physical attributes, as predicted in Table 1. Only three children in Study 2 had a reason for self-sorting, and these reasons also were simple and concrete.

Table 2 also presents coefficients (Pearson correlations, point bi-serial correlations, or Kendall Tau-B coefficients, depending upon the measurement scale of the respective variables) which reflect the relation between the children's ethnic knowledge and both age and language. Examination of the coefficients across studies indicates that the older children significantly more frequently used correct ethnic labels. Children who were Spanish-speaking more frequently knew their surname was Mexican, and used more ethnic role behaviors.

Table 2

The Percentage of Children Demonstrating Some Knowledge on Each and the Coefficients Relating Each Item with Age and Language for Studies 1 & 2

		Coefficients*	
Item or Scale	Knowledge Study 1/2	Age Study 1/2	Spanish-sp Study 1/2
Correct Ethnic Self-Label	29.1/37.0%	.38*/.26*	.46*/.22
Correct Ethnic Sorting	54.2/23.9	.29/.06	.08/.28*
Correct Self-Sorting	54.2/45.7	.16/-.10	.25/.20
Reason for Self-Sorting	33.3/6.5	.32/-.02	.53**/.06
Ethnic Constancy	45.8/37.0	.34/-.03	.25/-.01
Name Ethnic	41.7/28.3	-.15/.02	.34/.33*
Knowledge of Ethnic Behaviors	25.0/10.9	.05/-.09	.19/-.20
Use of Ethnic Behaviors	na/na	.28/-.06	.49**/.51***

*Pearson correlations when both variables are continuous, point biserial correlati there is one continuous and one dichotomous variable, and Kendall Tau-B coeffici both are dichotomous.
*p < .05. **p < .01. ***p < .001.
na = not applicable.

Kendall tau-B coefficients were computed to examine the relations among the ethnic items for the two studies. There was one cluster of items that were significantly interrelated and consistent across the studies: Correct Self-Sorting, Reason for Self-sorting, Ethnic Constancy, Family Ethnic, and Name Ethnic. That is, the children's scores on these measures were systematically related to each other such that children scoring high on one measure tended to score high on the other measures, and vice versa.

The assessment of the relationship between parents' background as measured by the Acculturation Rating Scale for Mexican Americans and children's ethnic identity indicated that, for this sample, there was little relationship between the parents' ethnic background or language and their child's ethnic identity. The only interesting finding was that the more assimilated the parents, i.e., the closer their cultural background was to that of the dominant Anglo society, the less likely their children were to group their Mexican classmates correctly ($r = -.31$, $p < .05$).

Conclusions and Implications of This Research

The results of Studies 1 and 2 are not directly comparable, particularly with respect to the ethnic grouping tasks and the Knowledge and Use of Ethnic Role Behaviors scales. However, for the most part, the outcome of the studies was similar.

The performance of these preschool children was consistent with our predictions about what children know about ethnic identity at this age. Their descriptions were simple and concrete, dealt with global observable characteristics that distinguish Mexican children, and when they could apply Mexican labels to themselves, these labels had little meaning. But the proportions of children who gave interpretable answers was not high; ethnic identity was just emerging in some of the children and not yet in others, and most had relatively little or no ethnic knowledge. Subsequent research has shown that, at the older age of 6 to 10 years, Mexican American children have more information about their ethnic group, and demonstrate increasing ability to label, group, and self-identify as Mexican, as well as to understand the permanence of their ethnicity. Their reasons for self-grouping as Mexican also are more abstract and trait-oriented, as predicted by the conceptual framework (Bernal, Knight, Garza, Ocampo, & Cota, 1990).

The lack of relationship between parents' ethnic background and their children's ethnic identity does not mean that the parents were not teaching them about their ethnic heritage; it may simply mean that many children were too young to understand even very basic ethnic concepts and characteristics. This conclusion is supported by the meagerness of the children's knowledge of their ethnic identity. It also is supported by the fact that older Mexican American children's ethnic identity has been found to be significantly related to parental ethnic background variables such as degree of preference for Mexicanism and generation of migration. Furthermore, relationships have been found between mothers' teaching their children about Mexican culture and some of the children's ethnic identity components (Knight et al, 1991).

One obvious educational implication of these results is that cultural teaching for comparable samples of young preschool children should dwell on very simple ethnic knowledge such as concepts, labels, and ethnic role behaviors. Comparable children of this age do not know much about their "Mexicanness" and neither understand the content of ethnic labels nor their social implications. While they may not be able to identify ethnic role behaviors (such as Mexican dances, songs, customs) as Mexican, learning how to engage in such behaviors can promote eventual associations between them and their ethnic group membership. An important limitation of the research is that the samples of this research were drawn from a low SES population of urban Denver families, and the results are not necessarily generalizable to Mexican children anywhere.

There is room for much research on ethnic identity in children, since it is only recently that mainstream developmental psychology has paid attention to the ethnic socialization of minority children in this country (Phinney & Rotheram, 1987). The future research plans of the present investigators are to extend their theory and methodology to youths, and to the broader conceptual framework of social identity theory (Tajfel, 1982). This framework includes ethnic identity, but also incorporates identities (e.g., gender identity, peer group identity) that have increasing relevance for adolescents, and that, in ethnic minority individuals, interact with ethnic identity. Longer term plans include research on the social identities of Mexican American youths in school settings with the goal of understanding the sociocultural processes involved in academic achievement.

References

Bernal, M. E., Knight, G. P., Garza, C. A., Ocampo, K. A., & Cota, M. K. (1990). The development of ethnic identity in Mexican American children. Hispanic Journal of Behavioral Sciences, 12, 3-24.

Cuéllar, I., Harris, L. C., and Jasso, R. (1980). An acculturation scale for Mexican-American normal and clinical populations. Hispanic Journal of Behavioral Science, 2, 199-217.

Domino, G., & Acosta, A. (1987). The relation of acculturation and values in Mexican Americans. Hispanic Journal of Behavioral Sciences, 9, 131-150.

Fischer, K. F. (1980). A theory of cognitive development: The control and construction of hierarchies of skills. Psychological Review, 87, 477-531.

Harter, S. (1983). Developmental perspectives on the self-system. In M. Hetherington (Ed.), Carmichael's manual of child psychology: Socialization, personality, and social development, (Vol. 4, pp. 275-385). New York: Wiley.

Knight, G. P., Bernal, M. E., Garza, C. A., Cota, M. K., & Ocampo, K. A. (in press). Family socialization and the ethnic identity of Mexican American children. Journal of Cross-Cultural Psychology.

Lewis, M., & Brooks-Gunn, J. (1979). Social cognition and the acquisition of self. New York: Plenum Press.

Montgomery, G. T., & Orozco, S. (1984). Validation of a measure of acculturation for Mexican Americans. Hispanic Journal of Behavioral Sciences, 6, 53-63.

Phinney, J. S., & Rotheram, M. J. (Eds.) (1987). Children's ethnic socialization: Themes and implications. Newbury Park: Sage Publications.

Selman, R. (1980). The growth of interpersonal understanding. New York: Academic press.

Acknowledgements

We extend our appreciation to Marty VanParys and Saneya Hassan for their scientific assistance. We are deeply grateful to the Central Denver Head Start Administration as well as to the directors and teachers of the centers that participated in this research. And, of course, we appreciate the voluntary cooperation of the parents and children who participated in this research. The warm hospitality and helpfulness of the Head Start settings in which this research was conducted greatly facilitated and encouraged this work.

Chapter V

Bernal and Martinelli

Use of the Role/Identity Procedure for Assessing Ethnic Identity in Mexican American High School Students

by

Kurt C. Organista
University of California, Berkeley

The purpose of this chapter is to report findings from a study (Organista, 1989) in which the role/identity procedure (Burke, 1980; Burke & Tully, 1977) was used to conceptualize and measure ethnic identity in Mexican American high school students. Analyses examining the relation between ethnic identity and psychological adjustment are also reported.

Conceptualization and Measurement of Ethnic Identity

Social scientists have described the content of self-concept as a multifaceted, organized collection of more specific identities (Burke & Tully, 1977; Rosenberg, 1979; Shavelson, Hubner & Stanton, 1976; Stryker, 1968). This conception helps to explain how a single person can have multiple definitions of self (e.g., adult, male, Mexican American, etc.). Presumably, identities vary in their importance to the individual and are thus organized into a hierarchy of salience.

At the top of the self-concept hierarchy are the most central, pervasive, and influential identities (e.g., age, gender, race) that influence most social interactions and help to organize other identities lower in the hierarchy (Burke & Tully, 1977). From this description of self-concept, ethnic identity emerges as a potentially influential identity in an ethnic individual's life experiences and self-conception.

Role/Identity Theory

Role/identities refer to meanings attributed to one's self that are associated with particular interactional settings or roles. The term *role/identity* is used to underscore what role/identity theorists view as the essential link between *identity* as the internal component of self and *role* as the external component. Burke and Tully (1977) maintain that role/identities do not stand in isolation but presuppose and relate to one or more counter-role/identities. For example, the role/identity "male" presupposes and relates to "female"; "minority" relates to "majority", and "Mexican American" relates to both "Anglo American" and "Black American".

The role/identity procedure. The role/identity procedure measures meanings attributed to self in a particular role and relates this role/identity to one or more counter-role/identities. Meanings attributed to self and roles are obtained by using a semantic differential instrument to make self-ratings and role-ratings on an arbitrary number of contrasting adjective pairs (e.g., Lazy/Hard-working). Each adjective pair is arranged on a scale ranging from one adjective (e.g., Lazy) to the other (e.g., Hard-working) so that a respondent can indicate where he or she believes self and roles fall on the continuum.

Next, a sample's conception of how a role and its counter-role differ is derived and then used to classify subjects into different role/identity types based on the similarity between the role and their self-ratings. This is accomplished through the use of the statistical procedure, discriminant function analysis, which allows the researcher to determine how differently two or more things (e.g., roles) are rated and which particular items (e.g., adjectives) are used to make these discriminations.

In the original validation study, Burke and Tully (1977) used the role/identity procedure to measure gender role/identity by having a sample of boys and girls make semantic differential ratings of themselves ("As a boy/girl I usually am..."), the role *boy*, and its counter-role *girl* (i.e., "Usually boys/girls are..."). Discriminant function analysis revealed that the sample did share a common conception of how the roles boy and girl differed. This conception was defined by the analysis which located a set of adjectives that were most used by subjects to discriminate the roles. In statistical terms, this set of adjectives is referred to as a function and can be thought of as a sample's set of stereotypes as to how they believe boys and girls to differ. This set of stereotypes was then used to classify subjects into "boy" or "girl" gender role/identity types by comparing their self-ratings to role-ratings on this set of stereotypes.

Results of the classification showed that 82% of the children were "correctly" classified as indicated from gender role/identity scores closer to the same sex role. However, 18% of the sample were "incorrectly" classified because they had gender role/identity scores closer to the role of the opposite sex. These two subject types were referred to as "same" and "cross" gender role/identity types, respectively.

Gender role/identity and self-esteem. Interestingly, Burke and Tully were able to infer from a subset of semantic differential ratings that "cross" gender role/identity types had lower self-esteem than "same" gender types. Cross gender types also reported more pressure and criticism for "inappropriate" gender role/identity (e.g., more likely to report being called "sissy", "homo", "tomboy", etc.) as compared to same gender role/identity subjects.

These findings suggested to this author that the role/identity procedure could be used to assess ethnic role/identity in Mexican Americans. Using the procedure, different ethnic role/identity types within a sample of Mexican Americans could be compared on multiple measures of psychological adjustment.

Using the role/identity procedure to assess ethnic/role identity in Mexican Americans. A potential problem with using the role/identity procedure to measure ethnic identity is that ethnic role/identity might be more difficult to assess than gender role/identity. This is because the role/identity procedure is designed to tap a common conception among subjects of how a role differs from its counter-role. Whereas boys and girls were found to have a common conception of how the roles boy and girl differed, members of different ethnic/racial groups (e.g., Mexican Americans and Anglo Americans) will probably be less likely to share a common stereotypes of how their respective roles differ. Studies which have examined how Mexican American and Anglos stereotype themselves and each other support this speculation (Buriel and Vasquez, 1982; Dworkin, 1976).

In the current study, the above predicament was resolved by performing separate discriminant function analysis on the role-ratings of Mexican American and Anglo American subsamples. It was predicted that each subsample would have its own unique conception of how the roles "Mexican American" and "Anglo American" differ. In addition to this modification, a third role, "Black American", was included in the ratings and analysis to see just how well subjects were discriminating the roles. An important advantage to these modifications was that Mexican American subjects could be classified into Mexican American (MA), Anglo American (AA), and Black American (BA) ethnic role/identity types once on the basis of their own group's stereotypes of these roles, and once again on the basis of the Anglo group's stereotypes.

It was predicted that Mexican American subjects classified as AA by the Mexican American functions would be lower in psychological adjustment than those classified as MA. This prediction was based on the assumption that having an ethnic identity similar to the group's conception of Anglo American will be more "inappropriate", and thus more related to stress, than having an ethnic identity similar to the group's conception of Mexican American.

It was also predicted that Mexican American subjects classified as MA by the Anglo functions would be less psychologically adjusted than those classified as AA. This prediction was based on Buriel's (1984) theory of cultural integration in which he posits that as acculturating Mexican Americans loose their culture of origin, they become more vulnerable to threats to sense of self (i.e. internalizing society's negative stereotypes of Mexican Americans) and to different forms of sociocultural maladjustment (e.g., academic maladjustment, delinquency, etc.). Such an "unprotected" ethnic sense of self, as Buriel refers to it, is operationalized in this study as being classified as MA by the Anglo functions, that is, having an ethnic identity based on Anglo stereotypes of what MAs are. Conversely, Mexican American subjects classified as AA by the Anglo functions are considered in this study to have a "protected" ethnic identity because they attribute the same favorable meanings to self as do Anglo subjects.

Method

Subjects

Subjects were 254 Chicano and 216 Anglo American high school students from a larger sample of 658 public high school students surveyed in three public high schools in Phoenix, Arizona. This sample had a mean age of 15.7 years (SD=.85 years), contained 318 males and 337 females (data missing for 3 subjects), and was composed of mostly tenth-grade sophomores (554 or 84.2%).

Procedures

Students were asked to participate in a study designed to examine how students view themselves, their school, and students from different cultural backgrounds. Participation was both voluntary and anonymous and students filled out survey batteries in their classrooms which contained the semantic differential and the measures of psychological adjustment. Students were instructed to make semantic differential ratings of themselves and the roles Mexican American, Anglo American, Black American, and Native American High School Student.

The latter two roles were included to prevent Mexican American and Anglo students from feeling like the exclusive focus of the study and to prevent members of the latter two groups from feeling excluded. Inclusion of these two roles was also designed to help Anglo subjects sharpen their ratings of the role Mexican American as a distinct minority group instead of just making more global minority/majority group distinctions in their ratings. Following role- and self-ratings, students completed four measures of psychological adjustment which are described below.

Dependent Measures

The Hopkins Symptom Checklist (Derogatis, Lipman, Rickels, Uhlenhuth & Covi, 1974) was used to assess psychological distress across five symptom dimensions: anxiety, depression, somatization, obsessive-compulsiveness, and interpersonal sensitivity[1].

The Rosenberg Self-Esteem Scale (Rosenberg, 1979) was used to assess global self-esteem. This scale has been used extensively by Rosenberg and others cited by Rosenberg to investigate self-esteem in huge samples of adolescent and minority high school students[2].

The Perceived Quality of Academic Life Scale (Okun, Kardash, Stock, Sandler & Bauman, 1986) was used to assess satisfaction with high school in such areas as classes, subject matter, teachers, personal progress, etc.[3] Although this scale was designed to assess satisfaction with college, it can easily be adapted to high school settings by substituting the term "high school" for "university" on the scale items (e.g., How do you feel about your education at this high school?).

Finally, a measure called the Ethnic-Related Stress Scale was created by the author to assess distress specifically related to ethnicity such as perceived prejudice, perceived tension between ethnic/racial groups at school, feelings of cultural marginality, etc.[4]

Results

Results of the discriminant function analyses performed on each subsample's role-ratings revealed that both Mexican American and Anglo American subsamples significantly discriminated the roles MA, AA, and BA high school student along two unique functions or sets of stereotypes. When three roles are rated, it is common for subjects to differentiate them along two functions, the first of which is the most discriminating.

The two functions calculated for Mexican American subjects had significant discriminatory power on the basis of both functions as indicated by a combined Wilk's lambda of .55. Lambda is an inverse measure of the discriminating power in the original variables. For Anglos, the two functions also had significant discriminatory power on the basis of both functions combined. In this case, there was a combined Wilk's lambda of .40.

Thus, both Mexican American and Anglo American subjects had their own unique conception of how the roles differed from one another. Deriving these conceptions involved interpreting each group's pair of functions. Basically, this involved examining how differently each group rated the three roles from each other and examining the specific sets of adjectives that subjects used to make these discriminations.

Mexican American stereotypes of MA, AA, and BA high school students. The biggest distinction that Mexican Americans made between the roles was one that differentiated the minority roles from the majority role. The Mexican American subsample's first set of stereotypes clearly differentiated AAs from the other two roles, but MAs and BAs were not much different from each other. An examination of the role-ratings for this set of adjectives suggested that this minority/majority group distinction was made primarily on the basis of those adjectives on which Mexican American subjects rated MAs and BAs higher than AAs on the characteristics *Tough* and *Athletic,* and lower than AAs on *Involved in politics, Ambitious,* and *Thinks a lot about the future.*

The second distinction Mexican Americans made between roles was one that characterized MAs as being distinct from BAs. The second set of adjectives distinguished MAs from both AAs and BAs but especially from BAs. An examination of role-ratings for this set of adjectives suggested that this MA/BA distinction was made primarily on the basis of those adjectives that showed MAs to be rated higher than BAs on the characteristics *Believes family life is important, Genuine, Modest,* and *Religious*; and lower than BAs on *Athletic* and *Modern.*

Anglo stereotypes of the roles MA, AA, and BA high school students. The largest distinction Anglo subjects made between roles was one that strongly differentiated AAs from MAs, and from BAs but to a lesser extent. This AA/MA distinction was made primarily on the basis of adjectives that showed AAs to be rated higher than MAs on the characteristics *Ambitious, Involved in politics, Thinks a lot about the future, Rational, Hard-working,* and *Athletic*; and lower than MAs on *Tough.*

The second distinction that Anglo subjects made was one that distinguished Blacks from both Anglos and Mexican Americans. This Black/non-Black distinction was based on a set of adjectives on which BAs were rated higher than AAs and MAs on the characteristics *Athletic, Tough, Assertive,* and *Musical.*

Classification of subjects into MA, AA and BA ethnic role/identity types. To classify subjects into different ethnic role/identity types, discriminant function scores were computed for each subject. Such scores were derived by multiplying each function's weighted set of adjectives by the subject's self-ratings on these same adjectives, and then summing across the products. The results of these calculations are numerical indices that were used to classify subjects into MA, AA, or BA role/identity types depending on the role to which their ethnic role/identity scores were most similar.

As can be seen in Table 1, the Mexican American discriminant functions classified 126 Mexican American subjects as MA, 77 as AA, and 27 as BA ethnic role/identity types. That is, most Mexican American subjects had ethnic role/identities most similar to their own group's stereotypes of what a Mexican American high school student is; a third had ethnic role/identities most similar to their group's stereotypes of what an Anglo American high school student is; and a few were most similar to their group's stereotypes of what a Black American high school student is (24 Mexican Americans were dropped from the analysis because of insufficient data). The Mexican American discriminant functions also classified 88 Anglo subjects as MA, 89 as AA, and 27 as BA (12 Anglo subjects were dropped from the analysis because of insufficient data).

The Anglo functions classified 36 Mexican American subjects as MA, 158 as AA, and 36 as BA. That is, most Mexican American subjects had ethnic role/identities most similar to how Anglo Americans rated themselves, while the rest were evenly divided into ethnic role/identity types most like the Anglo sample's stereotypes of MA & BA high school students. The Anglo discriminant functions also classified 34 Anglo subjects as MA, 147 as AA, and 23 as BA. That is, most Anglo subjects had ethnic role/identities most similar to their own group's stereotypes of Anglos, while a few had ethnic role/identity types most similar to their group's stereotypes of Mexican Americans and Blacks.

These findings indicate that the role/identity procedure was successfully used to classify Mexican Americans adolescents into different ethnic identity types on the basis of their own group's stereotypes and their Anglo peers' stereotypes. The question of how different ethnic identity types are within the Mexican American subsample was addressed by comparing them on various indices of psychological adjustment.

Ethnic role/identity and psychological adjustment. The relation between ethnic role/identity and psychological adjustment was investigated by comparing the scores of Mexican American subjects classified as MA, AA, and BA ethnic role/identity types on the four dependent measures of psychological adjustment. Anglo subjects were included in these analyses to observe whether the relation between ethnic role/identity and psychological adjustment for this subsample would be different than the relation predicted for the Mexican American subsample. These relations should differ between subsamples if the functions are classifying Mexican

Table 1

Classification of Subjects into Ethnic Role/identity Types by Mexican American and Anglo Discriminant Functions

	Discriminant Functions						
	Mexican American			Anglo American			
	Ethnic Role/identity			Ethnic Role/identity			
Subjects	MA[a]	AA[b]	BA[c]	MA	AA	BA	n
Chicanos	126	77	27	36	158	36	230
Anglos	88	89	27	34	147	23	204

Note. n size reflects number of subjects that completed self-ratings and could thus be classified.

[a] Mexican American Role/identity.
[b] Anglo American Role/identity.
[c] Black American Role/identity.

American subjects into meaningfully different ethnic role/identity types in a way that is unique to Mexican American subjects.

To accomplish this task, the statistical procedure Multivariate Analysis of Variance (MANOVA) was performed on the psychological adjustment scores of subjects. MANOVA allows researchers to compare two or more groups of subjects on several measures at the same time by detecting variance in scores within groups, between groups, and between group patterns of scores across several measures. Given two subsamples and three ethnic role/identity types, MANOVA was performed on psychological adjustment scores in a 2X3 Subsample (Mexican American, Anglo American) by Role/identity (MA, AA, BA) factorial design. MANOVA was performed once for subjects classified by the Mexican American functions and again for subjects classified by the Anglo functions.

Results showed no support for the prediction that Mexican Americans classified as AA would be less adjusted than those classified as MA on the basis of the Mexican American functions. Anglo subjects classified into ethnic role/identity types also did not differ in adjustment scores. In fact, the pattern of scores for Mexican Americans classified as MA, AA, and BA did not differ from the pattern of scores for Anglo Americans classified as MA, AA, and BA.

An overall difference in psychological adjustment was found between subjects classified as BA as compared to those classified as MA or AA as indicated by significant main effects for Role/identity, ($F(2,756)=3.34$, $p<.001$). In this MANOVA, a significant main effect for Role/identity indicates differences between role/identity types overall (i.e., combining both Mexican American and Anglo American subjects). Subjects classified as BA were found to be less satisfied with high school on the Perceived Quality of Academic Life than those classified as MA or AA, regardless of subsample. This finding was indicated by a significant univariate for the effect of Role/identity. A univariate effect in MANOVA conveys a difference on a particular measure.

Overall differences in psychological adjustment were also found between Mexican American and Anglo American subjects as indicated by a main effect for Subsample, ($F(1,377)=3.19$, $p<.01$). In this MANOVA a main effect for Subsample indicates an overall difference between the two subsamples. Mexican Americans were found to be higher in ethnic-related stress on the Ethnic-Related Stress scale and lower in self-esteem on the Rosenberg Self-Esteem scale as compared to Anglo subjects as indicated by significant univariates for these measures.

Results for subjects classified by the Anglo functions also revealed no support for the prediction that Mexican American subjects classified as MA by the Anglo functions would be lower in adjustment than those classified as AA. Again the pattern of scores for Mexican American classified as MA,

AA, and BA did not differ from the pattern of scores for Anglo Americans similarly classified.

Instead, an overall difference between subgroups was found that showed Mexican American subjects to be higher than Anglo subjects in ethnic-related stress. This was indicated by a significant main effect for Subsample, $F(1,379) = 2.77$, $p<.027$; with a significant univariate on the Ethnic-Related Stress Scale.

Discussion

The role/identity procedure adequately defined Mexican American and Anglo American conceptions of how Mexican, Anglo, and Black American high school students differ. The role Native American was not included in the analysis because it was not a focus of inquiry and also would have complicated the discriminant function analysis by adding a third counter-role/identity. For Mexican American subjects, the main distinction between roles was a perception of themselves and Blacks as being more tough and athletic than Anglos; perhaps in a poverty-enhanced, street-wise sense. Anglos were stereotyped as more ambitious, politically involved, and future oriented; perhaps in the traditional sense of striving towards the American dream.

The main distinction for Anglo American subjects was a perception of themselves as different from Mexican Americans along several dimensions on which they consistently rated Mexican Americans less favorably than themselves (e.g., lower on ambitious, hard-working, rational, future-oriented, politically involved, athletic, etc.). Hence, Anglo students perceived a sharper and wider distinction between themselves and Mexican Americans than did Mexican American students.

The secondary distinction made by Mexican American subjects was one in which they appeared to distinguish themselves as being more traditional than Blacks (e.g., more family-oriented, religious, and modest; less modern, etc.). The secondary distinction made by Anglo subjects was that of Blacks as being different than both themselves and Mexican Americans on the basis of popular stereotypes of Blacks (e.g., more athletic, musical, tough, etc.).

On the basis of the coherent stereotypes above, it was possible to use the role/identity procedure to classify subjects into MA, AA, and BA ethnic role/identity types. Most Mexican American subjects were classified as MA by their own group's stereotypes and as AA by the Anglo group's stereotypes. In contrast, most Anglo subjects were classified as AA by their own group's stereotypes but were equally classified as MA and AA based on the Mexican American group's stereotypes. These findings suggest that the majority of Mexican American subjects defined themselves as favorably as did Anglo subjects, and that the Mexican American group generally did not stereotype AAs more unfavorably than themselves.

The finding that Mexican American subjects classified into MA, AA, and BA ethnic role/identity types did not differ on any of the indices of psychological adjustment suggested that the content of ethnic identity, as assessed in this study, had no clear relation to psychological adjustment. Perhaps modifications made in adapting the role/identity procedure decreased its power to identify "protected" and "unprotected" types of ethnic identity. Also, the measures of psychological adjustment used might not have been specific enough to detect forms of distress more directly related to unprotective ethnic identity. There is also the question of how adequate the role/identity procedure is for assessing a subjective sense of ethnicity that is complex enough to be related to psychological adjustment.

Given the multiplicity of identities residing within an individual Mexican American, the specific influence of ethnic identity on psychological adjustment is likely to be subtle. One way of using the role/identity procedure to tease out this subtlety would be to include adjectival dimensions on the semantic differential that are likely to have a strong relation to psychological adjustment (e.g., Intelligent/Not intelligent, Physically Attractive/Unattractive, Responsible/ Irresponsible, Weak/Strong, etc.).

These types of dimensions were generally excluded in the current study because it was initially thought that they were too evaluative in nature (i.e., merely variations of the more general dimension Good/Bad) and would be related to psychological adjustment in ways not specific to ethnicity. However, these are exactly the kinds of stereotypic dimensions that have traditionally been used to differentiate ethnic minority groups from the majority culture. Therefore, future attempts to assess psychologically protective and unprotective types of ethnic identity might advance our knowledge by examining the role of such evaluative dimensions.

Another recommendation would be to explicitly assess self-in-role by having Mexican American subjects rate "As a Mexican American I usually am" as opposed to global self-concept (i.e., "Rate yourself"). The decision to assess global self-concept in the study reported was intended to minimize defensiveness on the part of subjects who might be sensitive about inquiries into their ethnicity, and to control for response biases such as making socially desirable ratings of self as a Mexican American. However, ratings of global self-concept may have tapped a more general sense of self than was desired.

As was described earlier, self-concept refers to the totality of multiple identities within a single person. Rosenberg (1979) uses the term global self-esteem to refer to overall self-regard with respect to global self-concept. These views of self-concept and self-esteem make it easy to understand how a person might feel negatively about a specific identity (e.g., ethnic identity) but positively about overall self. Therefore, self-ratings can vary depending on whether one is rating global self or a specific self-in-role. Hence, explicitly measuring self-in-role as a Mexican American will help to ascertain meanings attributed to self as an ethnic person.

One way to assess self-in-role as a Mexican American, without singling out Mexican American subjects, would be to have all subjects write in their ethnic background at the top of the semantic differential used to make self-ratings (e.g., "As a _____, I am..."). To maximize the accuracy of ethnic self-identification on the part of Mexican Americans subjects, they should first complete a questionnaire designed to specify their racial and ethnic background. Subjects could then be instructed to use their specific ethnic label from the questionnaire (e.g., Mexican American) to fill in the self-rating blank above.

Regarding inquiries into the relation between ethnic identity and psychological adjustment, care should be exercised in conceptualizing and assessing forms of distress that are most likely to be related to poor ethnic identity. For example, Burke and Tully (1977) found that "cross" gender role/identity subjects reported more criticism for "inappropriate" gender role/identity than did "same" gender role/identity subjects (e.g., more likely to be called derogatory names like "sissy", "homo", "tomboy", etc.). Analogous stressors could be assessed in the realm of ethnic identity. For example, certain ethnic identity types might be criticized by others for being too Anglo-oriented (e.g., "Not a real Mexican", "Tio taco" [Mexican American equivalent of Uncle Tom], etc.) or for being disloyal to the group (i.e., low ethnic pride and affiliation, uninvolved with "La Causa" or attempts to better the group, etc.).

The issue of ethnic loyalty should figure prominently in future attempts to conceptualize and assess ethnic identity. In an empirically derived model of Mexican American ethnicity, Keefe and Padilla (1987) identified two major dimensions of ethnicity which they call Ethnic Loyalty and Cultural Awareness. These dimensions were derived from a factor analysis of extensive survey data collected from a stratified random sample of Mexican Americans (N=381) from three different cities in California. Whereas Cultural Awareness refers to the external, objective dimension of ethnicity (e.g., language, knowledge of the history and culture of traditional and host cultures, etc.), Ethnic Loyalty refers to a personal, subjective sense of pride and preference for one cultural orientation over the other as manifested in self-identification, ethnic affiliations, perceived discrimination, etc.

Interestingly, Keefe and Padilla found that whereas Cultural Awareness gradually diminished across a span of four generations, Ethnic Loyalty remained constant. Hence, ethnic identity appears to become increasingly based on Ethnic Loyalty over time. As such, it may be degree of ethnic loyalty that determines how coherent a sense of ethnic identity is, and possibly how protective it will be against certain forms of psychological distress.

In a cluster analysis of their data, Keefe and Padilla were able to generate a typology of five distinct ethnic types based on varying degrees of Cultural Awareness and Ethnic Loyalty (e.g., high Cultural Awareness & average Ethnic Loyalty, low on both dimensions, etc.). While Mexican Americans as a group were found to maintain Ethnic Loyalty over time, certain individuals did not, and attention needs to be directed to how such individual-level fluctuations in Ethnic Loyalty affect the content and subjective meaning of ethnic identity.

Future uses of the role/identity procedure could address the above issue, and perhaps relate ethnic identity to psychological adjustment, by including semantic differential items designed to tap ethnic loyalty (e.g., Proud of Mexican background/Not proud of Mexican background, Prefer company of Anglo Americans/Prefer company of Mexican Americans, Believe Mexican Americans are discriminated against/Do not believe..., etc.).

Footnotes

¹Derogatis et al. (1974) reported coefficient alphas ranging from .84 to .87 (n=1435) for the five symptom subscales indicating uniformly high internal consistency. They also reported high test-retest reliability (one week time interval) for each subscale as indicated by coefficients ranging from .75 to .84 (n=425). Derogatis et al. (1974) reviewed several studies that showed high agreement between the five symptom dimensions and various clinical criteria including ratings of patients by psychiatrists, distress levels of nonpsychiatric outpatients, effects of psychotropic medication, etc.

²Rosenberg reported test-retest reliability coefficients of .85 and .88 in two small college samples administered the scale two weeks apart. A coefficient alpha of .80 was found in the current study, indicating satisfactory internal consistency, based on 567 of the high school students surveyed that completed the Rosenberg Self-Esteem scale. Rosenberg found his scale to correlate .30 with symptoms of depression and .48 with psychophysiological symptoms of anxiety in a sample of 5,024 high school students. Rosenberg also cited studies that found substantial correlations between his scale and other measures of self-esteem including the Coopersmith Self-esteem Inventory (.67) (Coopersmith, 1967) and a psychiatrist's ratings of 44 college students (.56).

³Okun et al. (1986) administered their scale to 121 community college students and 63 undergraduates and reported Cronbach alphas ranging from .74 to .86 indicating satisfactory internal consistency. They also reported adequate test-retest reliability (r=.70) over a two-week interval. With respect to validity, the authors reported significant correlations between their scale and the Quality of Education (r=.62, p<.001) and the Social Life (r=.23, p<.05) subscales of the College Students Satisfaction Questionnaire-Form C (Starr, Betz & Menne, 1983).

⁴The ERS had only marginal internal consistency among scale items as indicated by a coefficient alpha of .61. Coefficient alpha is a reliability coefficient used to assess multiple item additive scales.

References

Buriel, R. (1984). Integration with traditional Mexican-American culture and sociocultural adjustment. In J. L. Martinez, Jr. & R. H. Mendoza (Eds.), Chicano psychology (2nd ed., pp. 95-128). Orlando, Florida: Academic Press, Inc.

Buriel, R. & Vásquez, R. (1982). Stereotypes of Mexican-descent persons held by three generations of Mexican American and Anglo American adolescents. Journal of Cross- Cultural Psychology, 13, 59-70.

Burke, P. J. (1980). The self: Measurement requirements from an interactionist perspective. Social Psychology Quarterly, 43, 18-29.

Burke, P. J. & Tully, J.C. (1977). The measurement of role identity. Social Forces, 55, 881-897.

Coopersmith, R. (1967). The antecedents of self-esteem. San Francisco: Freeman.

Derogatis, L. R., Lipman, R. S., Rickels, K., Uhlenhuth, E. H., & Covi, L. (1974). The Hopkins Symptom Checklist (HSCL): A self-report symptom inventory. Behavioral Science, 19, 1-15.

Dworkin, A. G. (1976). National origin and ghetto experience as variables in the Mexican American stereotypy. In C. A. Hernandez, M.J. Haug, & N. N. Wagner (Eds.), Chicanos: Social and psychological perspectives (2nd ed., pp. 136-159). St. Louis, MO: C. V. Mosby Co.

Keefe, S. E. & Padilla, A. M. (1987). Chicano ethnicity. Albuquerque, NM: University of New Mexico Press.

Okun, M. A., Kardash, C. A., Stock, W. A., Sandler, I. N., & Bauman, D. J. (1986). Measuring perceptions of the quality of academic life. Journal of College Student Personnel, 27, 447-451.

Organista, K. C. (1989). The relation between ethnic identity and psychological adjustment in Chicano high school students. Unpublished doctoral dissertation. Arizona State University.

Rosenberg, M. (1979). Conceiving the self. New York: Basic Books.

Shavelson, R. J., Hubner, J. J. & Stanton, G. C. (1976). Self-concept: Validation of construct interpretations. Review of Educational Research, 46, 407-441.

Starr, A. M., Betz, E. L., & Menne, J. W. (1983). Manual: College student satisfaction questionnaire (revision). Ames, IA: Central Iowa Associates.

Stryker, S. (1968). Identity salience and role performance. Journal of Marriage and the Family, 4, 558-564.

Section III

Section III

Gender and Ethnic Identity

Social scientists have long recognized that there are differences in the socialization and life experiences of males and females. That these gender differences are manifested in their self-concepts and personal as well as social identities should come as no surprise. Ethnic identity may be one of the identities that is especially susceptible to gender differences, and the ways in which it is susceptible may range from subtle to very obvious. The implications of such differences for Mexican American high school youths and for Mexican American women are addressed in this section.

Gender and Ethnic Dimensions of Ethnic Identity in Adolescents

Patricia MacCorquodale stresses the importance of the effects of reflected appraisals from dominant group members on the self concept of minority group members, particularly Mexican Americans and females, and discusses the role that negative gender and race stereotyping may play in their self concepts. She first evaluates the relationship between ethnic labels and nativity, generation, and language use in a large sample of adolescent students. Then she examines the self-perceptions held by these students regarding their intelligence and self-confidence to determine if there are gender and ethnic differences in self concept. Finally, she assesses the role of the sources of reflected appraisals as determinants of gender and ethnic differences in intelligence.

Dilemmas of the High-Achieving Chicana

Judith Gonzalez focuses on a segment of the population of Mexican American women, those who are high achieving, upwardly mobile, and have a desire to advance themselves through education, and in addition are strongly identified as Mexican American. The value they place on their culture may lead such women to prefer males of their own ethnic background. Her concern is that such women may find themselves in a dilemma relative to their wish to form relationships with such men because they perceive that the Mexican American males in whom they might be interested do not necessarily regard them as desirable, and may feel threatened by high achieving women. This dilemma may lead to psychological distress, consisting of feelings of loneliness, lack of dates, and isolation from the larger ethnic community. In her chapter, Gonzalez attempts to find out whether women who are highly ethnically identified, prefer endogamy, and perceive that Mexican American males are threatened by high-achieving women, experience higher levels of psychological distress than women who are low on these characteristics.

Chapter 6: Identity: Gender and ethnic dimensions. P. MacCorquodale.

Chapter 7: Dilemmas of the high-achieving Chicana: The double-bind factor in male/female relationships. J. T. Gonzalez.

Chapter VI

Bernal and Martinelli

Identity: Gender and Ethnic Dimensions

by

Patricia MacCorquodale
University of Arizona

Charles Cooley (1902) characterized the self as a looking glass and thus began a tradition of conceptualizing the self as reflected. According to this characterization, the self develops from our interaction with others; that is, we come to see ourselves as we imagine others see us, in terms of reflected appraisals. A crucial assumption of this perspective is that individuals seek to establish stable identities and to evaluate them positively. Insofar as others provide information organized around gender and ethnicity, these characteristics will become important parts of identity.

The Nature of Identities

Sociologists differentiate personal from social identities (McCall and Simons, 1978). Personal identities are sets of categories unique to a particular individual, e.g. name and birth place. The configuration of unique characteristics that make up personal identity also includes social identities which refer to membership in groups, statuses and social categories, e.g. wife, physician, Protestant. As Stryker (1980) noted, people enter a world of categories and are immediately sorted into socially relevant categories. Societies, situations and groups vary in the extent to which they utilize and emphasize various categories. For example, religion may be an important consideration when inviting guests for a religious holiday dinner, but would not be used in assigning players to positions at a company baseball game.

The distinction between achieved and ascribed status is important in understanding social identities. Achieved statuses, such as occupation, are acquired through individual effort, knowledge and skills, so there is some competition between individuals for the position. Ascribed statuses, in contrast, are based upon inherited characteristics or positions that are acquired at birth or at a certain age. Ascribed statuses are important determinants of social interaction patterns and of access to many achieved statuses. Sex and age are the best examples of ascribed characteristics; we interact differently with a 17-year old male than an 80 year-old woman in our neighborhood. Similarly, each would have very different chances of getting a job with a sales company. The distinction between these types of statuses is not absolute but is a useful analytic tool.

In many societies, the physical characteristics that distinguish racial groups, such as color of skin and eyes, size and shape of the head, and facial characteristics, are used to ascribe racial status. Once individuals have been assigned to a racial category, which may also be attributed to ethnic groups, this differentiation acquires social meaning. Not only is membership in the group a social category, but various traits and behaviors that are deemed characteristic of the group are attributed to members of the group (Berscheid and Walster, 1978; Grant and Holmes, 1981; Hamilton, 1979). This process is called stereotyping. Stereotyping differs from other mental processes of categorization and generalization in that stereotypes emphasize negative characteristics of the group and are highly resistant to modification in the face of information that contradicts the stereotype. This process results in prejudice and discrimination (Katz, 1976; Stephan and Rosenfield, 1982; Wuthnow, 1982).

The consequences of this categorization for the individual are that a mental picture is evoked upon presentation of self and expectations are set before any interaction has occurred. Because social identities are derived from this reflected view of the self, ethnic identities are based upon the social meaning of ethnic categories.

Just as physical characteristics present racial and ethnic cues which structure social interaction, they also present information about gender. Gender categorization and the subsequent reflected self appraisals based upon it have important consequences. As Goffman (1977) noted, "every society seems to develop its own conception of what is 'essential' to, and characteristic of, the two sex classes" (p. 303). People assign individuals to a gender category on the basis of a small amount of information and then develop ways to ignore or explain away information that contradicts their stereotypes (Kessler and McKenna, 1978). Gender identity develops as individuals come to understand both their membership in a gender category and the social meaning attached to that categorization.

Socialization and Identities

Developmental studies indicate that age and gender are among the earliest distinctions that children learn (Kohlberg, 1966); racial identity is learned somewhat later but is fairly accurate by about the age of five (Greenwald and Oppenheim, 1968). Because gender, race, and ethnic categorization are important for the development of social identities, reflected appraisals organized around these categories reinforce their salience and stability. Comparisons across groups are necessary for minority group membership to be notable and distinctive (see McGuire and Padawer-Singer, 1976, on gender and Farris and Brymer, 1970, on ethnicity). Ethnic identity is related to several measures of acculturation including generation, language usage, and country of birth among adults (García, 1981) and adolescents (Buriel and Vasquez, 1982; Kagan and Knight, 1979; Lamare, 1982). Members of minority groups can develop negative self-concepts by internalizing the views of the majority group (Fanon, 1967; Rosenberg, 1965; Salgado de Snyder, 1987; Simmons, 1970); this has important consequences for academic performance (Wylie, 1979) and occupational choice (Rosenberg, 1965).

The effects of reflected appraisals from the dominant group on minority group members' self-concept are particularly important in childhood and adolescence for two reasons. First, taunting, name calling, and intergroup conflict, which highlight race and ethnic identities, are commonplace in many peer groups (Glock, Wuthnow, Piliavin and Spencer, 1975; Levinson, Powell and Steelman, 1986). Second, identity during childhood and adolescence relies heavily on ascribed characteristics because there is limited achievement upon which to base other identities (Farris and Brymer, 1970; Montemayor and Eisen, 1977; Rosenberg and Pearlin, 1978). Reflected appraisals based on gender and race and ethnic identities, however, do not affect self-esteem globally (see Franco, 1983; Gecas, 1973; Gordon, 1977; Larned and Muller, 1979; Porter and Washington, 1979; Rosenberg and Simmons, 1972; Wylie, 1979 on race and ethnicity, and Maccoby and Jacklin, 1974; O'Malley and Bachman, 1979 on gender). Instead, the feedback received from others focuses on specific dimensions of self-concept. Girls' orientation toward people and social approval, for example, contrasts with boys' orientation toward achievement and success (Rosenberg and Simmons; 1975); these differences may be related to career interests as well as vulnerability to criticism. The self-concept of Mexican American students who remain in high school is positively correlated with year in school (Franco, 1983) and is dominated by a greater concern with academic aspects of school than the self-concept of Anglo students (Farris and Brymer; 1970). Because reflected appraisals influence academic and occupational aspirations, this study will focus on two specific measures of competence: intelligence and self-confidence.

Conceptualization and Measurement of Ethnic Identity

This chapter conceptualizes ethnic identity as reflected in self-categorization according to ethnic labels and the meaning associated with the self-labels. For those of Mexican descent, ethnic identity is multidimensional and difficult to subsume under a single ethnic label (Buriel, 1987; Tienda and Ortiz; 1986) Ethnic identity, therefore, was measured by presenting a list of ethnic and racial categories and asking respondents "Which of the following would you use to describe yourself?" For the purposes of this chapter, we will focus upon those who responded Mexican, Mexican American, or White/Anglo. The identity Mexican American is more frequently chosen by those of Mexican descent than Mexican or Chicano (García, 1981; Gecas, 1973; Miller, 1976).

Systematic differences in self-concept between groups could be said to reflect either "real" differences in identity between groups or differential feedback based on group membership. For example, the view of girls as lacking skills in math and science could, theoretically, reflect their lower ability level or feedback from parents, peers, and teachers that girls aren't good in these areas. Because the evidence that identity patterns reflect "real" differences between gender or ethnic groups in abilities and skills is unconvincing (Frazier and DeBlassie, 1982; Wilkinson and Burke, 1984), this research assumes that systematic group differences in self-concept result from reflected appraisals. One reason that gender and ethnic groups may vary in competence may be that they rely upon different sources of reflected self-appraisals. Teachers and peers may be particularly important sources of stereotyped appraisals.

The goals of this chapter are three-fold. First, ethnic labels used by high school students will be studied with respect to nativity and language use. Second, self-perceptions as intelligent and self-confident will be examined in order to see if stereotyping has created gender and ethnic differences in self-concept. Third, we will turn to sources of reflected appraisals to determine whether differences in these sources account for gender and ethnic differences in self-rated intelligence.

The hypotheses explored in this research are as follows:

1. More of those who identify themselves as Mexican than Mexican American are expected to have been born in Mexico, to have parents born in Mexico, and to speak Spanish in the home.

2. Because gender and race stereotyping include low evaluations of intelligence, self-ratings of intelligence are expected to vary by ethnicity and gender, so that female and minority students will have lower ratings than males and Anglos.

3. Those who identify themselves as Mexicans will be affected more strongly by stereotyping and consequently give themselves lower ratings of intelligence than those who identify themselves as Mexican Americans.

4. Self-confidence is expected to vary by gender insofar as social stereotypes portray women as less competent, praiseworthy and able than men. Because ethnic stereotypes do not involve self-confidence, no significant variation by ethnicity is expected.

5. Gender and ethnic differences in perceived intelligence will be explained by sources of reflected appraisals; that is, when the importance of reflected appraisals is examined, gender and ethnic differences will be reduced. Teachers and peers as sources of reflected appraisals are expected to explain the gender and ethnic effects more than mothers and fathers (who are assumed to provide more personalized, less stereotyped feedback).

Method

Sample

The data used in this chapter were collected for a larger project on "Social Influences on the Participation of Mexican-American Women in Science" (MacCorquodale, 1984). In the spring of 1980 bilingual questionnaires were distributed to high school and junior high school students from a random sample of required classes stratified by grade level. This sampling design resulted in approximately equal representation from each grade (seventh through twelfth). A total of 2,442 questionnaires were completed, 3.7% in Spanish and 96.3% in English. The high response rate ranged from 87% to 99% across classes. Six schools in two school districts in southern Arizona were selected because they had a large representation from racial and ethnic groups. One district served a bordertown with a population of 12,000 and the surrounding rural area. The other, urban district served a city of 520,000 with a student population that was 35% minority. In the urban district, the two high schools with the largest proportion of minority students and the junior highs that serve them were selected for the study. Because this chapter focuses upon Mexican, Mexican American and Anglo students, 315 students (Blacks, Asian Americans, and Native Americans) were excluded from this analysis. As shown in Table 1, the subsample used in this analysis (n=2127) varied in urban or rural location and in socioeconomic class.

Two processes were used in developing the questionnaire. First, a review of the literature was conducted in order to determine the concepts of interest and to utilize existing questions and measures as much as possible. Second, an advisory board composed of Mexican American professionals (a scientist, engineer, psychologist, and social scientist) reviewed the questionnaire for cultural and linguistic bias and added variables they believed important for educational aspirations and achievement. The questionnaire was then pre-tested and discussed with ten students in order to determine that the instructions and wording of questions were clear and unambiguous. These procedures provided evidence of face validity; the measures used were either established and accepted in empirical research or conveyed a common understanding to advisory board members and students in the pretest. The resulting questionnaire included measures of educational and occupational aspirations, attitudes toward adult roles and school subjects, social support for education, background characteristics, and self-concept.

Measures

Self-concept. Self-concept was measured by asking students to indicate how they "picture themselves most of the time" on two items, intelligent and self-confident, presented in a semantic differential format. The two items were selected from a fifteen-item self-image scale developed by DeLamater and MacCorquodale (1979) from Sherwood's (1962) original scale. Because ethnic and gender identity are *not* related to global self-concept, the responses across items are not aggregated. Rather this chapter uses the two items, intelligent and self-confident, separately.

Mexican American Identity

Table 1

Background Characteristics of the Sample

School Attended	%	N
Urban District Junior Highs	20.9	445
Bordertown Junior High	13.4	285
Urban District Highs	38.6	820
Bordertown High	27.1	577
Father's Occupation		
Professional/White collar	26.8	570
Blue collar/Laborers	51.9	1105
No answer, deceased, unemployed	21.2	452
Father's Education		
Junior high or less	26.5	565
High school	35.7	760
Vocational/some college	12.2	260
College graduate/grad school	13.9	295
No answer, don't know	11.6	247
Mother's Education		
Junior high or less	30.3	646
High school	42.2	898
Vocational/some college	12.1	258
College graduate/grad school	9.0	194
No answer, don't know	6.3	134

Gender and ethnic identity. Gender and ethnic identities were measured by asking for students' self-categorization. For gender identity, students were asked whether they were male or female. As mentioned above, ethnic identity was measured by a question asking students how they would describe themselves. Six categories were presented: White/Anglo, Mexican American, Asian American, Black, Mexican, and Native American. In addition, students could check the "other" category and write in any label or combination of ethnicities. For the purposes of this chapter, students who checked Mexican are included in this category regardless of other identities they also checked (N=324). Fifteen percent of both the males and females chose this label. The remaining students who chose Mexican American or wrote in Mexican American with some other identity are classified as Mexican American (N=1312). Sixty-one percent of the males and 63% of the females chose this label. It is assumed that those who picked Mexican have a different sense of ethnic identity than those who used Mexican American. Those left who checked White/Anglo are included in that category (N=491) for a total of 2,127 respondents; 24% of the males and 22% of the females were included in this category. The White/Anglo students will be referred to as Anglos.

Nativity and language. To gather information about the social meaning of ethnicity, ethnic labels were compared with two other measures of ethnicity: nativity and language used in the home. Nativity referred to respondent's birthplace (United States, Mexico, other countries) and parents' birthplaces. A small number of respondents or their parents were born in Puerto Rico, Europe, Central or South America, coded as other countries. Responses to a question asking "What language is spoken in your home?" were categorized into three groups: usually Spanish; some Spanish and some English; usually English.

Sources of reflected self-appraisals. The sources of reflected self-appraisals were measured by inquiring about the importance of feedback from other people. Specifically, students were asked "how important is having these people think well of you?" Students rated evaluations from their mothers, fathers, teachers and friends according to whether these evaluations were very, quite, slightly, or not important. Those who were very important sources of reflected appraisals are referred to as significant others.

Analyses

Because the measures used in this study were primarily nominal or ordinal, analytic techniques using cross-classification were appropriate. In the cases of two-way cross-classification, chi-square (X^2) tests of significance were used on the resulting frequency distributions to determine if the association was significant. In the cases of three- or four-way cross-classification, log-linear techniques for categorical data were used (Fienberg, 1980; Knoke and Burke, 1980). Both of these techniques compare expected cell frequencies to observed frequencies, but chi-square uses proportions and log-linear uses odds (the ratio between the frequency of being in one category and the frequency of not being in that category). A comparison of two odds yields an odds ratio. Log-linear analysis is better suited to multidimensional cross-classifications than chi-square analysis because it simultaneously examines pairwise relationships, considers conditional relationships when other variables are present, and allows for interactions among the variables (Fienberg, 1980).

Log-linear analysis combines two important statistical tasks: building a model, and estimating the size of the effects that constitute the model. Model building begins with the simplest model--independence. It includes no effects of any variables on any others. Model building then proceeds through a succession of hierarchical models that are formed by adding effects to simpler models that form more and more complex models. The collection of effects in the ultimate "preferred model" represents all of the ways that one variable affects another. Each model in the hierarchical sequence from simple to complex has associated with it a set of expected frequencies--the counts we would expect to see in each cell of the table if the model were true. We gauge the discrepancy between observed ($\underline{f}$) and expected frequencies ($\underline{F}$) in a manner very similar to the familiar chi-square test.

The goal of model building is to find a preferred model that includes all of the significant interactions among the variables that make up the table. Once a preferred model has been built, the size of each effect that makes up the model is estimated by the use of odds ratios (see Fienberg, 1980, for formulas).

Results

Nativity

Ethnic identity was associated with respondent's and parents' birthplaces, as shown in Table 2. Among males, only 8.8% of those born in the United States described themselves as Mexican while 48% of those born in Mexico used this label. The label Mexican American appears to represent a blending of these two heritages; 61% of those born in the United States and half of those born in Mexico called themselves Mexican American. A third of the boys born in the United States and half of those born in other countries used the label White/Anglo. Because the pattern of results for females is essentially the same, they are not discussed separately.

Father's birthplace was associated with ethnic label for both boys and girls, as shown in Table 2. Among female respondents, 26% of those whose fathers were born in Mexico chose the label Mexican, as did 31% of the males. In contrast, 55% of the females with U.S.-born fathers and 73% of those with Mexican-born fathers described themselves as Mexican American. For males, very similar percentages were found. Thus, father's birth in Mexico was less likely to lead to using the label Mexican than respondent's birth in Mexico. Mother's birthplace was also associated with ethnic labels for male and female respondents in a pattern and to a degree that paralleled the results for father's birthplace; these results are not shown in Table 2. Because respondents' and parent's birthplaces were associated with ethnic labels, these results suggest that ethnic identity is, in part, influenced by nativity.

Generation

In order to determine whether the recency of immigration was related to ethnic identity, a measure of generation was computed from the information about respondents' and parents' birthplace. Respondents who were born outside of the United States were coded foreign born; they were the most recent immigrants to the United States. Those whose mother and/or father were born outside of the United States were first generation residents. If both the respondent and his/her parents were born in the U.S., they had been residents for two or more generations.

Mexican American Identity

Results

Nativity

Ethnic identity was associated with respondent's and parents' birthplaces, as shown in Table 2. Among males, only 8.8% of those born in the United States described themselves as Mexican while 48% of those born in Mexico used this label. The label Mexican American appears to represent a blending of these two heritages; 61% of those born in the United States and half of those born in Mexico called themselves Mexican American. A third of the boys born in the United States and half of those born in other countries used the label White/Anglo. Because the pattern of results for females is essentially the same, they are not discussed separately.

Father's birthplace was associated with ethnic label for both boys and girls, as shown in Table 2. Among female respondents, 26% of those whose fathers were born in Mexico chose the label Mexican, as did 31% of the males. In contrast, 55% of the females with U.S.-born fathers and 73% of those with Mexican-born fathers described themselves as Mexican American. For males, very similar percentages were found. Thus, father's birth in Mexico was less likely to lead to using the label Mexican than respondent's birth in Mexico. Mother's birthplace was also associated with ethnic labels for male and female respondents in a pattern and to a degree that paralleled the results for father's birthplace; these results are not shown in Table 2. Because respondents' and parent's birthplaces were associated with ethnic labels, these results suggest that ethnic identity is, in part, influenced by nativity.

Generation

In order to determine whether the recency of immigration was related to ethnic identity, a measure of generation was computed from the information about respondents' and parents' birthplace. Respondents who were born outside of the United States were coded foreign born; they were the most recent immigrants to the United States. Those whose mother and/or father were born outside of the United States were first generation residents. If both the respondent and his/her parents were born in the U.S., they had been residents for two or more generations.

Table 2

Ethnic Identity of Respondents by Nativity and Gender

Respondent's Birthplace:	U.S.	Mexico	Other
Males[a]	%	%	%
Mexican	8.8	48.5	12.5
Mexican American	60.7	50.9	37.5
White/Anglo	30.5	0.6	50.0
n	(820)	(163)	(8)
Females[b]			
Mexican	9.0	47.0	8.3
Mexican American	63.0	53.0	25.0
White/Anglo	28.0	0	66.7
n	(914)	(164)	(12)
Father's Birthplace:			
Males[c]			
Mexican	6.4	31.1	6.3
Mexican American	55.0	68.6	37.5
White/Anglo	38.6	0.3	56.3
n	(596)	(312)	(16)
Females[d]			
Mexican	8.1	26.2	20.0
Mexican American	54.8	72.9	36.0
White/Anglo	37.1	0.9	44.0
n	(642)	(336)	(25)

[a] $X^2=191.52$ with 4 d.f., $p<.001$ [b] $X^2=195.89$ with 4 d.f., $p<.001$
[c] $X^2=214.62$ with 4 d.f., $p<.001$ [d] $X^2=183.51$ with 4 d.f., $p<.001$

Table 3

Ethnic Identity by Generation and Gender

Gender	Foreign Born	First Generation	Second Generation
Males[a]	%	%	%
Mexican	46.8	12.9	6.9
Mexican American	50.3	81.4	51.8
White/Anglo	2.9	5.8	41.4
n	(171)	(295)	(570)
Females[b]			
Mexican	44.3	12.5	7.6
Mexican American	51.1	81.5	52.8
White/Anglo	4.5	6.0	39.6
n	(176)	(351)	(596)

[a] $X^2 = 310.32$ with 4 d.f., $p < .001$

[b] $X^2 = 296.38$ with 4 d.f., $p < .00$

Table 4

Ethnic Identity by Language Spoken at Home and Gender

Gender	English	English and Spanish	Spanish
Males[a]	%	%	%
Mexican	3.5	14.0	32.6
Mexican American	21.9	83.0	67.4
White/Anglo	74.6	3.0	0
n	(283)	(401)	(196)
Females[b]			
Mexican	3.7	15.0	36.8
Mexican American	20.7	83.2	62.5
White/Anglo	75.6	1.8	0.7
n	(299)	(559)	(152)

[a] $X^2 = 571.97$ with 4 d.f., $p < .001$

[b] $X^2 = 689.31$ with 4 d.f., $p < .001$

Table 5

Expected Frequencies for Two-Way Crosstabulations of Perceived Intelligence, Ethnic Identity and Gender Derived from Preferred Model[a]

	Intelligence		
	High	Medium	Low
Ethnic Identity			
Mexican	67	93	122
Mexican American	279	468	407
White/Anglo	155	203	117
Gender			
Male	265	369	257
Female	236	395	389

	Odds	
	High: Medium	Medium: Low
Ethnic Identity		
Mexican	.72	.76
Mexican American	.60	1.15
White/Anglo	.76	1.74
Gender		
Male	.72	1.44
Female	.60	1.02

[a] $L^2 = 3.83$ with 6 d.f. $p < .70$

Table 6

Expected Frequencies for Two-Way Crosstabulations of Perceived Self-Confidence, Ethnic Identity, and Gender Derived from Preferred Mo

	Self-Confidence		
	High	Medium	Low
Ethnic Identity			
Mexican	125	78	81
Mexican American	432	380	358
White/Anglo	138	185	149
Gender			
Male	346	324	210
Female	322	319	378

	Odds	
	High: Medium	Medium: Low
Ethnic Identity		
Mexican	1.60	.96
Mexican American	1.14	1.06
White/Anglo	.75	1.24
Gender		
Male	1.07	1.54
Female	1.01	.84

$^1L^2$ = 7.38 with 6 d.f., $p < .29$

Mexican American Identity

As evident in Table 3, generation was associated with ethnic idenity for both males and females. Forty-seven percent of the boys and 44% of the girls who are foreign born described themselves as Mexican compared to 12% of the first generation and 7% of the second generation residents. Again, the Mexican American label appears to blend current residence with cultural origins. Half of the foreign born and 81% of the first generation respondents of both sexes choose the identity Mexican American. As residence increased across the generations, there was a decreasing use of the identity Mexican and an increasing use of the label Mexican American or Anglo.

Language Use

Ethnic identity was also associated with language used in the home. As shown in Table 4, 33% of the males who spoke Spanish, 14% who spoke both languages, but less than 4% of those who spoke English labeled themselves Mexican. Similarly, 67% of the dominant Spanish speakers, 83% of the bilinguals, and 22% of the English dominant speakers called themselves Mexican American. The same pattern of association was found for girls. Thus, the use of Spanish in the home was associated with an increase in the likelihood of seeing oneself as Mexican for both boys and girls.

Intelligence

The preferred model for the cross-classification of self-rated intelligence, ethnic identity, and gender indicates that gender and ethnic identity had independent effects on intelligence. Students rated their intelligence on a five-point scale with intelligent labeled one and unintelligent labeled five. These five ratings were partitioned into three categories: high (1), medium (2), and low (3-5).

As shown in Table 5, in terms of ethnic identity, Anglos were more likely than minority students to rate themselves high on intelligence. Specifically, Anglos were 1.06 times more likely than Mexicans (.76/.72) and 1.3 times more likely than Mexican Americans (.76/.60) to rate themselves high compared to medium. Contrary to what was predicted, those who identified themselves as Mexican were 1.2 times more likely than Mexican Americans to rate themselves high in contrast to medium. Turning to the contrast between the medium and low categories, Anglos were 1.5 times more likely to be in the middle category than Mexican Americans and 2.3 more than Mexicans. Mexican Americans were 1.5 times more likely than Mexicans to be in the middle category. Thus, Anglos rated themselves higher than minority students on intelligence and, within the minorities, Mexicans were more likely than Mexican Americans to be in the highest and lowest categories. In terms of gender, boys were 1.2 more likely than girls to fall in the high rather than the medium category and 1.4 times more likely to be in the medium than the low category. Thus, the gender and ethnic differences that were expected were confirmed, i.e., boys described themselves as more intelligent than girls; Anglos rated themselves higher on intelligence than Mexican or Mexican American students.

Self-Confidence

In order to determine if gender and ethnic identity affected the other dimension of competence, we turn to the measure of self-confidence. The preferred model included independent effects of both gender and ethnic identity.

As shown in Table 6, self-confidence was similar to intelligence in its association with gender; in keeping with the social stereotypes, girls were less self-confident than boys. Boys were slightly more likely than girls to be in the high than the medium category, but nearly twice as likely than girls to have rated themselves in the middle compared to the low categories. However, the association with ethnic identity diverged from that found for intelligence. Minority group members rated themselves higher on self-confidence than those from the majority group. Mexicans were 2.1 times more likely than Anglos and Mexican Americans 1.5 times more likely than Anglos to rate themselves high rather than medium in self-confidence. Comparing the Hispanics, students who identified themselves as Mexican were more likely than Mexican Americans to place themselves in the high than the medium self-confidence category. At the other end of the scale, however, Anglos were 1.3 times more likely than Mexicans and 1.2 times more likely than Mexican Americans to rate themselves in the medium as compared to the low categories of self-confidence. Thus, Mexican descent students are overrepresented in the highest and lowest categories of self-confidence. That self-confidence and intelligence vary in their association with ethnic identity affirms the decision to examine the self-concept measures separately.

Sources of self-appraisals

The final issue is whether the sources of reflected self-appraisals account for the gender and ethnic differences in perceived intelligence. Is it that feedback from teachers has more importance for girls than boys or that Hispanic students place more stress on parents than do Anglo students? These questions required a four-way cross-classification. If gender or ethnic identity was not significant in these models, then the sources of reflected self-appraisals would explain the gender or ethnic difference. Similarly, models with interactions would indicate that the sources are more important with respect to intelligence for some students than for others.

For all four sources of reflected self-appraisals, the preferred model included separate effects of gender, ethnic identity and the importance of the source; this means that the importance of appraisals from teachers, friends, mother and father does *not* explain gender and ethnicity differences in intelligence. All three are needed. In all cases, if the source was rated as very important, students rated themselves higher on intelligence. When teacher or friends were very important, the likelihood that students would rate themselves in the high rather than medium category increased 1.7 times. When father was very important, the odds were 3.5 times greater of rating oneself high compared to the middle category, and for mother, the odds increased 2.2 times. Parents and teachers, however, also appeared to be sources of negative appraisals for students. Where parents and teachers were important, students were more likely to be in the low in contrast to the medium category than when these sources were less important. The models for father and mother, however, must be considered cautiously; the model for mothers did not fit as well as the others, and the distributions on both was very skewed because nearly everyone rated their parents as very important.

Discussion

This chapter has shown that the categories of ethnic identity were related to nativity, generation, and language use in this sample of high school students. Those who were born in Mexico or had parents who were born in Mexico were more likely to describe themselves as Mexican than those native to the United States. Similarly, those who were Spanish dominant were more likely to choose Mexican than those who were bilingual or English dominant speakers. These differences between Mexicans and Mexican Americans provide support for our hypothesis that these ethnic labels reflected different meanings. Part of the meaning attached to the ethnic label appears to include information about social origins, i.e., respondent's birthplace and his or her parents' birthplace. Additionally, the continuity of ethnic ties and traditions, as indicated by speaking Spanish at home, may form some of the content of ethnic identity. Studies of the subjective meaning of these labels are needed to substantiate this interpretation.

The examination of self-ratings of intelligence and self-confidence revealed important sex and ethnic variations in self-concept. As expected, boys and Anglos rated themselves as more intelligent than girls and minority group members. Minority girls were doubly disadvantaged insofar as their self-concepts as intelligent were reduced by both their gender and ethnicity. Since, as discussed above, there is no convincing evidence from other studies that supports "real" differences between sex and ethnic groups in intelligence, these differences may be derived from the content of reflected appraisals. That is, if Anglos and Mexicans were not inherently different in intelligence, the discrepancy in feedback given to majority and minority group members may be the source of these self-concepts. These findings suggest that gender and ethnicity continue to be powerful cues that evoke stereotypes and structure social interaction. Further research into the content of reflected appraisals should examine whether minority students and girls receive more derogatory comments about their intelligence than do majority students or boys.

That reflected appraisals do not affect self-concept globally was indicated by the finding that minority students rated themselves *higher* in self-confidence than majority students. Among minority students, Mexicans gave themselves higher ratings than Mexican Americans. That self-confidence was stronger among those who labelled themselves Mexican could be due to the importance of confidence in the Mexican value system; foreign-born Mexican Americans were more likely than native-born Mexican Americans to see themselves as proud and well adjusted (Dworkin, 1970). Alternatively, like other minority groups, they may have developed self-confidence as an outcome of ethnic pride efforts that have attempted to revitalize or reaffirm ethnicity (Smith and Foley, 1978; Steinberg, 1981). Ethnic pride may be particularly important in the context of this study; the schools used in this research are located in southern Arizona close or adjacent to the border where minority groups are often larger numerically than majority groups.

That sources of reflected appraisals do not explain differences in intelligence was indicated by the separate effects of gender, ethnic identity and sources on intelligence. Thus, it is *not* differences in the importance of teachers, friends, mother and father to boys or girls, Hispanics or Anglos which explain differences between these groups in intelligence. When others were rated as very important, students saw themselves as more intelligent. This suggests that feedback from significant others provides information about one's own intelligence and that significant others can affect self-perception of students *regardless* of gender or ethnicity. This research suggests that teachers and friends can be particularly important sources of positive feedback about intelligence and that increases in their importance to students will improve self-perceived intelligence. Mother and fathers were also important sources of evaluations; however, they are unlikely to become more important as nearly everyone rated them highly. Other sources of feedback, such as siblings, the media, and neighbors, deserve attention along with the content of feedback from specific sources.

Some Conclusions

This chapter has explored various ethnic identities that are salient in the Southwest and the meanings attached to them. Future research should attend to three issues: 1) the importance of the categories used to measure ethnic identity, especially in Hispanic populations where a variety of labels are used; 2) the subjective meaning attached to these labels; 3) the strength of ethnic identity. Of particular interest would be the connection between ethnic identity and ethnic traditions, such as ethnic food, celebrations of holidays and religious events, and knowledge of ethnic history, and ethnic ties as evident in patterns of social interaction and friendship networks. Second, this chapter examined differences in self-rated intelligence and self-confidence by gender and ethnic identity; girls and minority students see themselves as less intelligent than boys and majority students. Because these group differences conform to social stereotypes, these findings suggest that reflected appraisals vary by gender and ethnicity. Social stereotypes about self-confidence concern gender but not ethnic identity, and, in this study, girls are less self-confident than boys. That Mexican students have higher self-confidence than Mexican American or Anglo students reinforces the importance of studying the self as a multidimensional rather than as a global phenomena. Further work is particularly needed on the positive reflected appraisals provided by ethnic group membership and the affective or emotional dimensions which may be particularly salient to the subjective sense of self. Intelligence and self-confidence are the foci of this work because they are relevant to high school students; the connection of these and other characteristics to educational and occupational achievements needs to be documented in some detail.

This chapter also examined the sources of reflected appraisals. That valuing the evaluations of others increases self-ratings of intelligence validates our belief that other people provide significant sources of information about the self, and that these sources may provide an alternative view to the social stereotypes prevalent in society. Since differences in self-rated intelligence persist even when sources of reflected appraisals are introduced, attention should be turned to the content of feedback from these and other sources. Perhaps salient feedback mirrors the social stereotypes about the intelligence of women and minorities, or the positive information provided by significant others is insufficient to contradict the negative messages from other sources. The importance of educators to students from ethnic and racial minority groups suggests that teachers, counselors and other school personnel *potentially* can provide positive feedback to minority students which would help counter the stereotypes that dominate the media and other institutions. Finally, we need to explore more directly the content of the reflected appraisals and how individuals piece together feedback from disparate sources. Studying the role of various significant others in reflected appraisals would have practical consequences which may reduce the extent to which the educational system perpetuates inequities based on gender and ethnicity, as well as conceptual implications for our understanding of the interplay between schools and families.

References

Berscheid, E., & Walster, E. (1978). Interpersonal attraction (2nd edition). Reading, MA: Addison-Wesley.

Buriel, R. (1987). Ethnic labeling and identity among Mexican Americans. In J. S. Phinney and M. J. Rotherman (Eds.) Children's ethnic socialization (pp. 134-152). Beverly Hills, CA: Sage.

Buriel, R. & Vasquez, R. (1982). Stereotypes of Mexican descent persons: Attitudes of three generations of Mexican-American and Anglo-American adolescents. Journal of Cross Cultural Psychology, 13, 59-70.

Cooley, C. H. (1902). Human nature and the social order. New York: Scriber's.

DeLamater, J., & MacCorquodale, P. (1979). Premarital sexuality. Madison, WI: University of Wisconsin Press.

Dworkin, A. G. (1970). Stereotypes and self-images held by native-born and foreign-born Mexican Americans. In J. H. Burma (Ed.), Mexican-Americans in the United States (pp. 397-409). Cambridge, MA: Schenkman.

Fanon, F. (1967). Black skin, white masks. New York: Grove.

Farris, B., & Brymer, R. A. (1970). Differential socialization of Latin and Anglo-American youth: An exploratory study of self-concept. In J. H. Burma (Ed.), Mexican-Americans in the United States (pp. 411-25). Cambridge, MA: Schenkman.

Fienberg, S. E. (1980). The analysis of cross-classified categorial data (2nd ed.). Cambridge, MA: MIT Press.

Franco, J. (1983). A developmental analysis of self-concept in Mexican-American and Anglo school children. Hispanic Journal of Behavioral Sciences, 5, 207-218.

Frazier, D. J. & DeBlassie, R. R. (1982). A comparison of self concept in Mexican-American and non-Mexican American late adolescents. Adolescence, 17, 327-334.

García, J. (1981). Yo soy Mexicano...: Self-identity and sociodemographic correlates. Social Science Quarterly, 62, 88-98.

Gecas, V. (1973). Self-conceptions of migrant and settled Mexican Americans. Social Science Quarterly, 54, 579-595.

Goffman, E. (1977). The arrangement between the sexes. Theory and Society, 4, 301-331.

Glock, C.Y., Wuthnow, R., Piliavin, J. A., & Spencer, M. (1975). Adolescent prejudice. New York: Harper & Row.

Gordon, V. (1977). The self-concept of Black Americans. Washington, D.C.: University Press of America.

Grant, P. R., & Holmes, J. G. (1981). The integration of implicit personality theory schemas and stereotype images. Social Psychology Quarterly, 44, 107-115.

Greenwald, H. J., & Oppenheim, D. B. (1968). Reported magnitude of self-misidentification among Negro children--artifact? Journal of Personality and Social Psychology, 8, 49-52.

Hamilton, D. L. (1979). A cognitive-attributional analysis of stereotyping. In L. Berkowitz (Ed.), Advances in experimental social psychology: Vol 12 (pp. 53-81). New York: Academic Press.

Kagan, S. and Knight, G. (1979). Cooperation-competition and self esteem: A case of cultural relativism. Journal of Cross Cultural Psychology, 10, 457-467.

Katz, P. (Ed.) (1976). Towards the elimination of racism. New York: Pergamon Press.

Kessler, S., & McKenna, W. (1978). Gender: An ethnomethodological approach. New York: John Wiley.

Knoke, D. & Burke, P. J. (1980). Log-linear models. Beverly Hills, CA: Sage Publications.

Kohlberg, L. (1966). A cognitive developmental analysis of children's sex-role concepts and attitudes. In E. Maccoby and C. Jacklin, The development of sex differences (pp. 82-173). Stanford: Stanford University Press.

Lamare, J. W. (1982). The political integration of Mexican-American children: A generational analysis. International Migration Review, 16, 159-188.

Larned, D. T. & Muller, D. (1979). Development of self-concept in Mexican-American and Anglo students. Hispanic Journal of Behavioral Sciences, 1, 279-285.

Levinson, R., Powell, B. & Steelman, L. C. (1986). Social location, significant others and body image among adolescents. Social Psychology Quarterly, 49, 330-337.

Maccoby, E., & Jacklin, C. (1974). The psychology of sex differences. Stanford: Stanford University Press.

MacCorquodale, P. (1984). Social influences on the participation of Mexican-American women in science. Final Report to the National Institute of Education. ERIC ED 234 991.

McCall, G. J., & Simons, J. L. (1978). Identities and interactions. New York: Free

Press.

McGuire, W. J., & Padawer-Singer, A. (1976). Trait salience in the spontaneous self-concept. Journal of Personality and Social Psychology, 33, 743-754.

Miller, M. V. (1976). Mexican Americans, Chicanos, and others: Ethnic self-identification and selected social attributes of rural Texas youth. Rural Sociology, 41, 234-247.

Montemayor, R., & Eisen, M. (1977). The development of self-conceptions from childhood to adolescence. Developmental Psychology, 13, 314-319.

O'Malley, P. M., & Bachman, J. G. (1979). Self-esteem and education: Sex and cohort comparisons among high school seniors. Journal of Personality and Social Psychology, 37, 1153-1159.

Porter, J. R., & Washington, R. E. (1979). Black identity and self-esteem: A review of studies of Black self-concept. Annual Review of Sociology: Vol 5, 53-74.

Rosenberg, M. (1965). Society and the adolescent self-image. Princeton: Princeton University.

Rosenberg, M., & Pearlin, L. I. (1978). Social class and self-esteem among children and adults. American Journal of Sociology, 84, 53-77.

Rosenberg, M., & Simmons, R. G. (1972). Black and white self-esteem: The urban school child. Washington, D.C.: American Sociological Association.

Rosenberg, M., & Simmons, R. G. (1975). Sex differences in the self-concept of adolescence. Sex Roles, 1, 147-159.

Salgado de Snyder, V. N. (1987). The role of ethnic loyalty among Mexican immigrant women. Hispanic Journal of Behavioral Sciences, 9, 287-298.

Sherwood, J. J. (1962). Self-identity and self-actualization: A theory and research. Unpublished doctoral dissertation, University of Michigan, Ann Arbor.

Simmons, O. (1970). The mutual images and expectations of Anglo-Americans and Mexican-Americans. In J. H. Burma (Ed.), Mexican-Americans in the United States (pp. 383-395). Cambridge, MA: Schenkman.

Smith, W. E. & Foley, D. E. (1978). Mexicano resistance to schooling in a south Texas colony. Education and Urban Society, 10, 145-176.

Steinberg, S. (1981). The ethnic myth. Boston: Beacon.

Stephan, W. G. & Rosenfield, D. (1982). Racial and ethnic stereotypes. In A. G. Miller (Ed.), In the eye of the beholder (pp. 92-136). New York: Praeger.

Stryker, S. (1980). Symbolic interactionism: A social structural version. Menlo Park, CA: Benjamin/Cummings.

Tienda, M. & Ortiz, V. (1986). "Hispanicity" and the 1980 census. Social Science Quarterly, 67, 3-20.

Wilkinson, S. M. & Burke, J. P. (1984). Ethnicit6y, socioeconomic status and self concept: Effects on children's academic performance. Journal of Instructional Psychology, 11, 203-210.

Wuthnow, R. (1982). Anti-semitism and stereotyping. In A. G. Miller (Ed.), In the eye of the beholder (pp. 137-187). New York: Praeger.

Wylie, R. (1979) . The self-concept: Vol 2. Theory and research on selected topics. Lincoln: University of Nebraska.

Chapter VII

Dilemmas of the High Achieving Chicana:

The Double Bind Factor in Male/Female Relationships

by

Judith Teresa González
California State University, Fresno

This exploratory study focuses on the relationship between ethnic identification, endogamy, perceptions that Chicano males are threatened by female achievements, and psychological distress. A strong sense of ethnic identification, coupled with a preference to marry within one's own ethnic group, presents a "double bind" for the high achieving Chicana. This "double bind" is the tension between strong ethnic identification and preference toward endogamy combined with the perception that males are threatened by high achieving women. Psychological distress is the hypothesized outcome of this "double bind." This distress, as measured by self-reported level of stress related to feelings of loneliness, lack of dates, and sense of isolation from a larger ethnic community, is significantly higher than that of less ethnically identified cohorts in the study. Ethnic identification is defined as friendship preferences and operationalized as the reported proportion of close friends who are Chicano. Preferred endogamy is the preference to date and marry other Chicanos. This study attempts to answer a basic question: does the combination of high ethnic identification, preferred endogamy and perceptions that high achievements pose a threat to Chicano males lead to significantly higher levels of psychological distress?

Ethnic Identification

This work defines ethnic identification as a preference for close friendships within one's own ethnic group. Other dimensions of ethnic identification, such as dietary preferences, language preference, and self-labeling, may play a role in ethnic identification as well. These were not chosen for two reasons: (a) the present study is a secondary analysis of existing data, thus necessitating the use of available measures, and (b) this definition of ethnic identification is behaviorally consistent with the concepts used by other behavioral scientists studying ethnicity and ethnic identity (Arce, 1981; García, 1982; Rothman, 1960; Smith, 1980; Tajfel, 1974). Also, language preference is not always a valid indicator of ethnic identification, as monolingual English speaking Mexican Americans may retain high ethnic identification.

Exogamy vs. Endogamy

The selection of a marriage partner is an important decision seldom made without consideration of educational and social compatibility (Burgess & Wallin, 1943; Centers, 1949; Glick, 1958, 1960; Hollingshead, 1950; Thomas, 1951; Udry, 1966; Warner & Srole, 1945). For an ethnically identified individual, marriage choice may entail consideration of a partner from the same ethnic group.

Endogamy is the preference to marry within one's own ethnic group. While upward social mobility and acculturation are positively associated with exogamy (outmarriage) as opposed to endogamy (Griswold del Castillo, 1984; Murguia, 1982), there are other influences on endogamy. It is likely that strong ethnic identification will short circuit the marked tendency to outmarry (Fernandez & Holscher, 1984; Murguia, 1982) among highly educated Chicanos. There are several reasons why this might be the case. First, the advent of the Chicano Movement during the 1960-1970s has increased ethnic consciousness among young, college-age Mexican Americans, which is likely to result in a return to strong in-group orientations. Secondly, the relative scarcity of Mexican American students on college campuses reinforces ethnic boundaries (Barth, 1969; Hayes-Bautista, 1974; Royce, 1982). Thirdly, Arce (1981) shows that Chicanos tend to shed lower class value orientations with upward mobility, but retain ethnic identification. Similarly, Gans (1965) noted that first and second generation Italians in Boston generally disapproved of exogamy, in spite of rapid upward mobility during the early 20th century.

While upward mobile Chicanas may prefer educated Chicano males, this preference is problematic if male and female concepts of women's family role are in conflict. Studies focused specifically on Hispanics' sex role stereotyping and gender identity substantiate that traditional concepts of women's family role persist among educated males (Gonzalez, 1982; Triandis, Marin, Hui, Lisansky, & Ottati, 1984). The Gonzalez (1982) study showed that Mexican American males were more likely to agree with the appropriateness of the sex-role stereotypes than were Anglo males. Overall, males were more likely than females to report that these sex role stereotypes reflected appropriate behavior. Hawley and Even (1982) found that a lag existed between Mexican American males and females regarding appropriate male and female roles. Women thought that sex roles should be more egalitarian than did their male counterparts across all educational groupings, although differences were less marked between the more highly educated men and women. This research indicates that Chicano males are more likely to believe that women should retain traditional sex role behaviors, thus leading to possible conflict between the sexes' notions of appropriate role behavior. Furthermore, more highly educated and acculturated Hispanic women (Baca-Zinn, 1978, 1980; Buriel & Saenz, 1980; Espin & Warner, 1982; Harris, 1979; Kranau, Green, & Valencia, 1982; Ortiz & Santana-Cooney, 1984; Soto, 1982, 1983; Soto & Shaver, 1982; Zeff, 1982) favor balanced decision making and equal roles in conjugal relationships. Zeff (1982), using the Bem Sex Role Inventory, found that Chicanas viewed themselves as less stereotypically feminine than either Black or Anglo women. In essence, highly educated Chicanas may experience conflict between their perceptions and males' perceptions of appropriate sex role behavior.

Psychological Distress

For the high achieving Chicana who prefers to marry within her own ethnic group, the choice of a partner is complicated by several factors. As discussed above, one factor could be ideological incompatibility with regard to appropriate sex roles. Additionally, upwardly mobile Chicanos tend to marry outside of their ethnic group (Bean & Bradshaw, 1970; Fernandez &

Holscher, 1984; Murguia, 1982) and men tend to outmarry slightly more frequently than women (Griswold del Castillo, 1984). Finally, the relatively small number of college educated Chicano males (Tomas Rivera Center Sourcebook, 1986; U.S. Bureau of the Census, 1980) further shrinks the pool of available partners. A dissonance between endogamy and a possible shortage of compatible marriage partners may possibly lead to psychological distress, as depression is related to being single (Roberts & Roberts, 1982; Vega, Warheit, & Meinhardt, 1984).

Hypotheses of This Study

It is not possible to draw causal inferences from these current data regarding a specific link between endogamy, perceived threat, and psychological stress. Based on the framework presented, an association is hypothesized between perceived threat and higher levels of psychological distress among ethnically identified and endogamous Chicanas. This perceived threat stems from a perception that males are threatened by women's educational achievements. This positive association is not expected to hold for Chicanas who are not endogamous or ethnically identified.

Method of the Research

Sampling. Data were obtained from a project entitled "Chicanas in Postsecondary Education," sponsored by the Center for Research on Women at Stanford University conducted during the 1980-81 academic year. Both male and female Chicano students from five California colleges were randomly selected to participate in the study. Colleges ranged in selectivity from a private university to an open-door admissions community college. Two California state colleges, one in a predominantly rural area and one in a major metropolitan area, were among the five campuses. Another was a selective university within the University of California system. The sampling frame was a list of Spanish surname students who had self-identified as Mexican American obtained from the Registrar's office at each campus, except for the urban State University. At that university, the research team selected all Spanish surname students from microfiche records and used residence as a filter in doubtful cases where Spanish surname students were possibly not Mexican origin. A stratified random sample of students based on year in college was selected from these lists.

Selected students were sent a questionnaire containing a battery of items tapping their academic and social experiences as college students.

Items included attitudes toward marriage, dating, participation in Anglo and Chicano organizations, presence of academic, social, and financial stress, and ethnic identification items. Students who did not respond to the first questionnaire were sent two reminder postcards and another questionnaire following the reminder postcards. The research team hired campus liaisons to contact students who did not respond to the mailings through personal phone calls, yielding 22 more respondents. The final response rate was 55.9%, for a total of 679 participants in the study, 508 of which were females. For the present study, only females were selected. Some comparisons to the males will be made with respect to levels of endogamy and perceived threat later in this paper.

A brief description of the respondents shows that these students were slightly older (mean age = 23) than the traditional college age student and were overwhelmingly single (75%).

Operationalization of the Variables

Ethnic identification. Ethnic identification is represented by associational preferences. Associational preferences are operationalized using the reported proportion of close friends that are Mexican American and frequency of seeking Mexican American friends to discuss personal concerns or problems. Endogamy is operationalized as preferring to date and marry other Chicanos.

Associational preferences. To measure associational preferences, two items were used. These asked respondents (a) to state which percentage of their closest friends were Mexican or Mexican American and (b) how often they discussed problems with these friends. Respondents were assigned an item score of "0" if they had less than 50% Mexican American friends and an item score of "1" if they had 50% or more Mexican American friends. If respondents reported that they at least "frequently" discussed problems with these friends, they were given an item score of "1," otherwise, they were assigned a "0." When summed together, item scores provided a range of 0-2 on ethnic identification. These scores are presented in Table 1.

Table 1

Summary Statistics for Ethnic Identification Scale

Score	% of total	% of females	% of males
0 = No criteria met	39.9	40.7	37
1 = 50%+ Chicano friends	25.9	25.0	27
2 = 50%+ Chicano friends and frequently discuss personal problems	34.2	34.3	35
n	679	508	16

Note. ns do not add to 679 due to 11 missing cases on sex identifier.

Table 2

Factor Analysis of Endogamy and Perceived Threat Items

	Mean	S.D.	Endogamy Factor Loading	Threat Factor Loading
When a Chicana marries, it is important for her to marry within her own ethnic group	2.35	1.20	[.65]	.13
I almost always date Chicanos(as)	2.70	1.34	[.89]	-.04
It is important for me to make life better for Chicanos	4.07	.89	[.35]	.00
Chicanos tend to exclude Chicanas in political and organizational activities	2.62	.97	.00	[.44]
Chicanos tend to be frightened by educated Chicanas	2.91	1.17	.09	[.70]
Because of our college degree we are going to be viewed as elitists by less educated Chicanos	3.01	1.11	.01	[.39]
Eigenvalues			1.82	1.47
Percent of total variance			30.3%	24.5%
Variance of two factors combined			54.8%	

Bracketed items under each category are the component items for the respective factor.

Results of the Study

Endogamy and threat measures. Preference for endogamy and perceptions that males were threatened by women's accomplishments were measured by a series of 5-point Likert items in the original questionnaire that tapped attitudes toward dating, marriage, contribution to the betterment of life for Chicanos, Chicana female participation in campus organizations, and perceptions of male attitudes toward educated Chicanas. Items with their respective factor loadings and original item means and standard deviations are illustrated in Table 2. The first factor refers to preferred endogamy. The second factor is "perceptions of threat."

Psychological distress. As discussed earlier, psychological distress is self-reported negative stress stemming from social isolation. The original questionnaire contained 13 6-point Likert items assessing distress. Responses ranged from "this is not stressful" to "extremely stressful." Factor analysis revealed three distinct factors: (a) academic, (b) financial, and (c) psychological distress. Psychological distress was measured by 4 Likert items among the 13 original items. These included (a) reported intensity of negative stress relative to lack of dates, (b) being in a cold social environment, (c) lack of a cohesive Chicano community, and (d) feeling lonely. These items showed respective factor loadings of .59, .61, .31, and .73. Item means ranged from 1.76 for the item "lack of cohesive Chicano community" to 2.76 for the item "being in an atmosphere where people are cold and unfriendly." Standard deviations ranged from 1.33 to 1.73. Generally, students were not extremely distressed, as evidenced by the low means.

Scales to measure perceived threat, level of preferred endogamy, and psychological distress were created by converting the original items to Z-scores, weighting them by the factor loadings and then summing the weighted items. The scale means for (a) perceived threat, (b) level of preferred endogamy, and (c) psychological distress for females were: .0002, .0627, and .0296 respectively.

Correlations. The zero-order correlation matrix in Table 3 shows the relationship between preferred endogamy, perceived threat, and psychological stress for the entire female sample. In support of the hypothesis, there was a significant correlation between perceived threat and distress ($r = .19$; $p < .001$ for the female sample).

Table 3

Zero-Order Correlations for Endogamy, Perceived Threat, and Psychological Stress

	Endogamy	Threat	Distress
1. Endogamy		.15*	.10*
2. Threat			.19***
3. Distress			

*p < .05   ***p < .001   n = 467

To test the basic hypothesis, we examine specific profiles of women based on combinations of ethnic identification and preferred endogamy. First, the original ethnic identification measure was recoded so that women scoring "0" or "1" were considered as low in ethnic identification; those scoring "2" were high. The endogamy scores were subdivided at the median; those below the median were "low endogamy"; others were "high endogamy." From these divisions, four distinct profiles were created: high on both ethnic identification and endogamy; high on ethnic identification, but low on endogamy; low on both; and low on ethnic identification but high on endogamy. The results showed that the positive correlation between perceived threat and stress was statistically significant for those high on both ethnic identification and endogamy, but for none of the other three groups (r = .19, p < .009; all others ns). These data imply that only a combination of high ethnic identification and preference toward endogamy will lead to a corresponding association between perceived threat and psychological distress. If one is not both ethnically identified and endogamous, perceived threat is not associated with distress. Table 4 shows the results of this analysis.

Table 4

Correlations Between Perceived Threat and Psychological Stress for Selected Profiles of Ethnic Identification and Level of Endogamy

		Ethnic Identification	
		Low	High
Level of Endogamy	Low	.07 ns n = 125	.16 p < .06 n = 165
	High	.06 ns n = 47	.18 p < .009 n = 165

Stepwise regression analysis was also performed. The first step included all predictors, i.e., ethnic identification, perceived threat, and preferred endogamy, resulting in an R^2 of identification, resulting in no change in the R^2. Final results showed that all predictor variables accounted for less than 4% of the variance in psychological distress, a modest finding. Respective standardized betas for ethnic identification, perceived threat, and endogamy were -.03, .12, and .10. Standard errors were .05 for all predictors. The strongest predictor of psychological distress was perceived threat.

Male/female comparisons. An interesting set of ancillary questions arise when considering male gender identity. Do men agree with the women's impressions that achievements imply threat? Are men equally endogamous? Do men experience equal amounts of psychological distress? This study explores in brief these questions comparing the male subset of the sample (N = 160) with the females. The single item responses of the constituent threat scale were compared between men and women. There were significant gender differences with respect to the perception that Chicano males are frightened by educated Chicanas. Women scored significantly higher than the men, respective means were 3.00 and 2.62 (t = -3.52, p < .0001). There is significant disparity between male and female perceptions of the degree of threat posed by women's accomplishments. The findings are contrary to previous research showing men lagging behind women in endorsement of more expansive role behavior. There were no significant differences between Chicano males' and females' perceptions that men excluded women from participation in political and campus activities or that college educated Chicanos would be viewed as elitists. Respective means were -.0022 for men and .0002 for women (t = -.03; ns).

T-tests comparing males and females showed no difference between males and females regarding preference to date and marry other Chicanos. Contrary to the literature that documents higher distress among women, there were no differences in psychological distress.

Discussion of the Results

Disparity Between Men and Women

The disparity between Chicano male and female perceptions of threat was a most intriguing finding. Chicano men say they are not threatened by women's accomplishments, yet the women think they are. Either the men are reluctant to report their true feelings, or there are some serious gaps of understanding between the sexes. If women's perception that men are threatened by female accomplishment is overplayed, as this study implies, the conflict could really be stemming from inability for men and women to communicate effectively. If, however, women's views are not distorted, the "double bind" constitutes a significant social dilemma.

There is strong evidence to suggest that men and women do not talk, but rather compete. In doing so, they may read mixed signals from each other, especially if competition occurs in an intimate relationship. Pleck (1973) conducted an experiment among male and female college dating partners where they were instructed to play a sentence completion game as a pair. Men who had been classified as "threatened" by successful females were more likely to compete with their partners in the game. The other men were more likely to cooperate so the team could win. There is an implied causal force that may explain the discrepancy in perceptions between the men and women. It is possible that both men and women justify their competitive behavior by holding certain perceptions of each other.

In a situation where competition takes place, women are likely to sense that the man feels threatened, and may experience exacerbated threat due to the exigencies of a competitive situation. Conversely, in a competitive situation, the man will view the woman as a threat rather than as a potential mate. Outside of the situation, the man may underplay the intensity of felt threat.

The threatened men in Pleck's study were also more likely to report preferring to date women who appeared less confident, i.e., less threatening. Because Mexican culture places a high emphasis on the man as the dominant partner (Penalosa, 1968) in a conjugal relationship, highly confident and competitive women may pose an even greater threat than for Anglo men. However, because the contemporary Chicano conjugal relationship (Baca-Zinn, 1982) demonstrates a marked pattern of dual decision making, the gap between ideal and real can be narrowed by underplaying one's emotional reaction of threat. Hence, men may actually feel more threatened than they are willing to admit.

The significant relationship between perceived threat and psychological distress is another interesting finding. The correlation is low enough to suggest that there may be other factors at play in causing distress. The "double bind" does not seem to be an overwhelmingly strong factor in distress. The modest amount of variance accounted for by the three predictor variables suggests that other factors are affecting psychological distress. Other factors not measured in the study, such as individual coping strategies or cognitive appraisal of threat, may be affecting psychological distress. Recent work (Vega, Warheit, & Meinhardt, 1988) suggests that women deploy varying coping mechanisms to deal with strain in conjugal relationships, and that coping factors as well as cognitive dispositions mediate between strain and consequent levels of depression. It is possible that the Chicanas vary in their cognitive orientations and coping strategies enough to cause disparity between their perceptions and reality as men see it. Therefore, any given Chicana could hold a negative perception of threat and thus experience distress even when men do not actually feel threatened by their achievements. Further research is warranted to examine cognitive styles, coping mechanisms, and distress among professional Chicanas both within and outside conjugal relationships.

Additionally, it is possible that feelings of distress are responses to alienation or social isolation from the mainstream college environment. This isolation, in turn, could produce a drive toward ethnic cohesion and endogamy. A recent study by Segura (1989) documents the high level of alienation and loneliness felt by Chicana and Mexican immigrant women who were employed in jobs traditionally held by white females. These women also reported experiencing a greater sense of belonging and camaraderie with other Chicanas in the work place. Alternatively, increased contact between Mexican American college men and women might possibly result in conflict, as both have increased opportunities for discussion and disagreement regarding sex role expectations. Such conflict could then lead to higher distress.

There are several ways that partners might react to the "double bind." Firstly, experiencing distress might become painful enough to force the woman's decision to forego her own education and personal achievements to attain marriage goals. Conversely, the attainment of educational and career goals may disrupt current marriages, requiring new choices and hard negotiation. Other options might include a decision to remain single, marry outside of the ethnic group, or work with one's partner to attain support. No choice is without effort or discomfort; each requires a redefinition of what is considered an appropriate balance in male/female relationships.

Clearly, this work points to the need to initiate serious dialogue between the sexes and to embark upon further research in the area of Chicano sex role perceptions as they differ between men and women.

Methodological Weaknesses

The post-hoc nature of the data limits theory building. The study of stress and distress in particular is plagued by inconsistent definitions of what constitutes stress (Munoz, 1986; Whitman, Spendlove, & Clark, 1986) and its concomitant emotional states. Future research should consider the use of a validated, reliable psychological distress measure such as the CES-D. Future study of the conflict between culturally prescribed sex role behavior and professional role behavior among high achieving Mexican American women should include more items dealing directly with male gender identity and threats to male status in conjugal relationships. This future study should also include variation with respect to ethnic identification and educational and occupational attainment, to ascertain if differences in gender identity are affected by ethnic identification and social class within the Mexican American culture.

The current findings have immediate policy implications for counseling practice. The most important of these is the development of new group and individual counseling strategies. If the combination of strong ethnic identity, endogamy, and perceptions that female achievements threaten males leads to psychological distress, therapist should be sensitive to issues of insecurity or threat that may emerge during therapy. Further research into coping strategies and decisions made by Chicanas regarding marriage could be applied to relationship skills building courses. Formation of peer support groups to redefine sex roles, break down misperceptions, and reinforce effective coping skills is one way to deal with distress (Maslach, 1982; Whitman, Spendlove, & Clark, 1986). Modeling of effective coping strategies and frank discussion of the issues that emerge during courtship and in marriage could be applied as foci to cross-sex and women's support groups.

Conclusion

The data provoke further study into the process of sex role socialization that occurs in contemporary Mexican American families. As Chicana women continue to achieve professional status, they will continue to struggle with integration of their own female role behavior into the work world. Perhaps it can be argued that highly educated, professional Chicanas are marginal members of both ethnic and professional role groups. College educated, professional Chicanas are still relatively scarce in numbers, and are struggling to maintain an ethnic identity in the face of long held sex role expectations. They experience conflict as their behavior is changing more rapid than their sex role attitudes and the attitudes of their male counterparts. Their professional and academic obligations place them squarely in the dominant society's work world; yet many of their values regarding marriage choices and appropriate sex roles originate in the world of their parents and family. Chicanas are marginal in two ways: vis-a-vis their ethnic reference group and vis-a-vis the dominant society's work world. Further research would guide action aimed at breaking this uncomfortable "double bind."

Mexican American Identity

Acknowledgements

The larger project of which this work is a part was sponsored by the Center for Research on Women, Stanford University, and funded by the Ford Foundation, 1980-81. Acknowledgments to Dr. John A. García, Coordinator of Research at the Mexican American Studies and Research Center, University of Arizona and to Dr. David Torres, Management and Policy Department, College of Business and Public Administration, University of Arizona, for their helpful comments and critique of this paper.

Note: Acknowledgment is given for permission to reprint an updated version of this article which originally appeared in Sex Roles: A Journal of Research, 7/8, May 1988, 367-380.

References

Arce, C. (1981). A reconsideration of Chicano culture and identity. Daedalus, 110, 171-191.
Baca-Zinn, M. (1975). Political familism: Toward sex role equality in Chicano families. Aztlan, 6, 13-26.
Baca-Zinn, M. (1978). Chicano family research: Conceptual distortions and alternative directions. Journal of Ethnic Studies, 7, 57-71.
Baca-Zinn, M. (1980). Employment and education of Mexican American women: The interplay of modernity and ethnicity in eight families. Harvard Educational Review, 50, 47-61.
Barth, F. (1969). Ethnic groups and boundaries. Boston: Little, Brown, and Company.
Bean, F. D., & Bradshaw, B. S. (1970). Intermarriage between persons of Spanish and non-Spanish surname: Changes from the mid-nineteenth to the mid-twentieth century. Social Science Quarterly, 51, 389-395.
Burgess, E. W., & Wallin, P. (1943). Homogamy in social characteristics. American Journal of Sociology, 49, 109-124.
Buriel, R., & Saenz, E. (1980). Psychocultural characteristics of college-bound and non-college-bound Chicanas. Journal of Social Psychology, 110, 245-251.
Centers, R. (1949). Marital selection and occupational strata. American Journal of Sociology, 54, 530-535.
Espin, O. M., & Warner, B. (1982). Attitudes toward the role of women in Cuban women attending a community college. International Journal of Social Psychiatry, 28, 233-239.
Fernández, C., & Holscher, L. M. (1984). Chicano-Anglo intermarriage in Arizona: 1960-1980: An exploratory study of eight counties. Hispanic Journal of Behavioral

Sciences, 5, 291-304.
Gans, H. J. (1965). The urban villagers. NY: The Free Press.
García, J. A. (1982). Ethnicity and Chicanos: Measurement of ethnic identity, identification, and consciousness. Hispanic Journal of Behavioral Sciences, 4, 295-314.
Glick, P. C. (1958). American families. NY: John Wiley and Sons.
Glick, P. C. (1960). Intermarriage and fertility patterns among persons in major religious groups. Eugenics Quarterly, 7, 31-38.
González, A. (1982). Sex roles of the traditional Mexican family: A comparison of Chicano and Anglo students' attitudes. Journal of Cross Cultural Psychology, 13, 330-339.
Griswold del Castillo, R. (1984). La familia: The Chicano family in the urban Southwest: 1848 to the present. South Bend, IN: University of Notre Dame Press.
Hawley, P., & Even, B. (1982). Work and sex-role attitudes in relation to education and other characteristics. Vocational Guidance Quarterly, 31, 101-108.
Hayes-Bautista, D. (1974). Becoming 'Chicano': A 'disassimilation' theory of transformation of ethnic identity. (Unpublished doctoral dissertation, University of California).
Hollingshead, A. B. (1950). Cultural factors in the selection of marriage mates. American Sociological Review, 15, 619-627.
Kearl, M. C., & Murguia, E. (1984). Age differences of spouses in Mexican American intermarriage: Exploring the cost of minority assimilation. Social Science Quarterly, 65, 453-460.
Kranau, E. J., Green, V., & Weber, G. V. (1982). Acculturation and the Hispanic woman: Attitudes toward women, sex-role attribution, sex-role behavior, and demographics. Hispanic Journal of the Behavioral Sciences, 4, 21-40.
Maslach, C. (1982). Burnout–The cost of caring. Englewood Cliffs, NJ: Prentice-Hall.
Muñoz, D. G. (1986). Identifying areas of stress for Chicano undergraduates. In M.A. Olivas (Ed.), Latino college students. NY: Teacher's College Press.
Muñoz, D. G., & García-Bahne, B. (1977). A study of the Chicano experience in higher education (Grant No. MN24597-01). Washington, D.C.: The Center for Minority Group Mental Health Programs, National Institute of Mental Health.
Murguia, E. (1982). Chicano intermarriage: A theoretical and empirical study. San Antonio, TX: Trinity University Press.
Ortiz, V., & Santana-Cooney, R. (1984). Sex role attitudes and labor force participation among young Hispanic females and non-Hipanic white females. Social Science Quarterly, 65, 392-400.
Peñalosa, F. (1968). Mexican family roles. Journal of Marriage and the Family, 30, 680-689.
Pleck, J. H. (1973). Male threat from female competence: An experimental study in college dating couples. (Unpublished doctoral dissertation, Harvard University).
Reed-Sanders, D., Dodder, R. A., & Webster, L. (1985). The Bem Sex-Role Inventory across three cultures. Journal of Social Psychology, 125, 523-525.
Roberts, R. E., & Roberts, C. R. (1982). Marriage, work and depressive symptoms among Mexican Americans. Hispanic Journal of Behavioral Sciences, 4, 199-221.
Rothman, J. (1960). In-group identification and out-group association: A theoretical and experimental study. Journal of Jewish Communal Service, 37, 81-93.
Royce, A. P. (1982). Ethnic identity: Strategies of diversity. Bloomington, In: Indiana University Press.
Segura, D. (1989). Chicana and Mexican immigrant women at work. Gender and

Society, 3, 37-52.
Selye, H. (1974). Stress without distress. Philadelphia: Lippencott.
Selye, H. (1976). The stress of life. NY: McGraw-Hill.
Smith, T. W. (1980). Ethnic measurement and identification. Ethnicity, 7, 78-95.
Soto, E. (1983). Sex role traditionalism and assertiveness in Puerto Rican women living in the United States. Journal of Community Psychology, 11, 346-354.
Soto, E., & Shaver, P. (1983). Sex-role traditionalism, assertiveness, and symptoms of Puerto Rican women living in the United States. Hispanic Journal of Behavioral Sciences, 4, 1-19.
Tajfel, H. (1974). Social identity and intergroup behavior. Social Science Information, 13, 65-93.
Thomas, J. L. (1951). The factor of religion in the selection of marriage mates. American Sociological Review, 16, 487-491.
The Tomás Rivera Center, a National Institute for Policy Studies. (1986). The changing profile of the Mexican American: A sourcebook for policy making. Claremont, CA: Author.
Triandis, H. C., Marin, G., Hui, C. H., Lisansky, J., & Ottati, V. (1984). Role perceptions of Hispanic young adults. Journal of Cross-Cultural Psychology, 15, 297-320.
Udry, J. R. (1966). The social context of marriage. Philadelphia, PA: J. B. Lippencott Co.
U. S. Bureau of the Census. (1980). Table 150, Southwestern states (Arizona, California, New Mexico, Texas, and Colorado).
Vásquez, M. (1982). Confronting barriers to the participation of Mexican American women in higher education. Hispanic Journal of Behavioral Sciences, 4, 147-165.
Vega, W., Kolody, B., & Valle, R. (1988). Marital strain, coping, and depression among Mexican American women. Journal of Marriage and the Family, 50, 391-403.
Vega, W., Warheit, G. J., & Meinhardt, K. (1984). Marital disruption and prevalence of depressive symptomatology among Anglos and Mexican Americans. Journal of Marriage and the Family, 11, 817-824.
Warner, W. L., & Srole, L. (1945). The social systems of American ethnic groups. New Haven, CT: Yale University Press.
Whitman, N. A., Spendlove, D. C., & Clark, C. H. (1986). Increasing students' learning: A faculty guide to decreasing stress among students (ASHE-ERIC Higher Education Reports, No.4).
Zeff, S. B. (1982). A cross-cultural study of Mexican American, Black American, and White American women at a large urban university. Hispanic Journal of Behavioral Sciences, 4, 245-261.

Section IV

Bernal and Martinelli

Section IV

Social Policy

In this last section attention shifts from in-group perspectives to consider Mexican American's ethnic identity in a broader societal context. Unquestionably, research on ethnic identity must move from the realm of the individual and ethnic group to examine issues related to the larger society, since ethnic groups do not exist in isolation.

Perceptions of Mexican Americans Across Time

Aware that students represent future leaders in American society, Gordan addresses the question of how Mexican Americans are viewed by college students. Gordon utilizes longitudinal data to examine the opinions of college students regarding Mexican Americans at two points in time. In addition, his research replicates studies done of college students' views of other major ethnic groups extending back over 50 years. These data give a clear view of the changes over time that have taken place in students' views of ethnic groups, and of where Mexican Americans fit into the spectrum of groups.

From the perspective of this chapter it is important to be aware of the influence that members of the core group have on the ethnic identity of Mexican Americans. Widely held negative stereotypes of an ethnic group can lead to negative self-concepts for individuals and a reluctance to identify with that group. In the case of Mexican Americans, the presence of persistent negative images found in samples of students in the Southwest points to the need to carefully evaluate the potential effects of these biased views.

Ethnic Identity and Policy Implications

García's focus, like Gordon's, is on the broader implications of ethnicity and how the larger society affects Mexican Americans. His attention is given to the way in which ethnic identity, in an instrumental sense, influences public policy. To examine the relationship between ethnic identity and policy he first addresses issues relating to the conceptualization and measurement of ethnic identity. He explores the current debate over the salience of ethnicity in modern society and attempts to understand its persistence. García raises several measurement concerns, such as the need for researchers to ascertain the role of behaviors in the operationalization of ethnic identity.

Moving into the public realm, he delves into the role of ethnic identity in ethnic group mobilization. He discusses six areas that are relevant in the ability of an ethnic group such as Mexican Americans to be effective in policy arenas. Finally, García specifies the link between ethnic identity and public policy, which he sees related to the social psychological roots of ethnic identity and its dynamic nature. Ethnic identity serves as a community resource base, aids in defining group goals, and helps to mobilize group members on specific issues. All of these functions make ethnic identity a critical variable in understanding dominant/minority group relations.

Chapter 8. College students' perceptions of ethic identity: The case of Mexican Americans. L. Gordon.

Chapter 9. Ethnic identity research and policy implications for Mexican Americans. J. A. García.

Mexican American Identity

Chapter VIII

Bernal and Martinelli

College Student Perceptions of Ethnic Identity: The Case of Mexican Americans

by

Leonard Gordon
Arizona State University

A number of studies in recent years have demonstrated the continuing importance of ethnic identity in American society. Study projects as diverse as Glazer and Moynihan's (1963) in New York City and Martinelli's (1984) in Scottsdale, Arizona have demonstrated the salience of ethnic identity on the personal behaviors, family patterns, and institutional life of many people. Consequently, an initial consideration regarding Mexican Americans, as the central focus of this article, is to explore the nature of ethnicity and its broad consequences for all ethnic groups in contemporary pluralistic American society.

In sociology, the theoretical school of symbolic interactionism holds that ethnic identity is a consequence of both intra- and intergroup processes (Blumer, 1969). For an ethnic group such processes encompass a variety of ethnic characteristics. These would include internal group developments of cultural historical memories, the nature of basic ethnic familial, religious, educational, economic, and political institutional life forms, the degree of cohesiveness of the ethnic group, and the self-perceptions and depth of meaning such perceptions have on members of the ethnic group toward their own ethnicity. All of these factors are influenced to some degree by the perception members of other ethnic groups have of a given ethnic group.

The nature of ethnic identity is also influenced when an ethnic group is a numerical and status minority in relation to one or more other ethnic groups, as in the case of Mexican Americans. Then the positive or negative stereotypical perceptions of the group, and behaviors based on those perceptions, become a large factor in the formation and activation of ethnic identity (Lieberson, 1961). The kind of substantial consequences of general stereotypical perceptions on Mexican American ethnic identity are made evident by the well tested Thomas Theorem (Thomas, 1931). As first documented in studies of Polish immigrants into American society, the theorem holds that beliefs about ethnic groups, whether accurate or false, lead to real consequences. The early century negative stereotypes of Polish children led to a self-fulfilling prophecy of negative self-perceptions and lower achievement among Polish children. This process has been documented more recently to lead to negative self-perceptions and lower academic performance levels of Mexican Americans, Blacks, and other minorities in public schools (Rosenthal and Jacobson, 1968).

Given this conceptual and research tested background on the effects of stereotypes on ethnic identity, it is of interest to examine college student perceptions of Mexican Americans. The interest in such perceptions is in terms of the implications for the future. College students represent a high proportion of future societal leadership. Past studies, extending over a half century, show a behavioral relationship between collegiate student stereotypical perceptions and their subsequent behaviors toward various racial and ethnic groups (Gordon, 1986). In turn, the attitudes and behaviors ethnic group members experience have a major effect on their own ethnic identity and how they relate to their own ethnic group and others.

It is with these consequences in mind that the findings of this chapter are reported. There are substantial implications respecting the future of intergroup conflict, conflict resolution, and/or cooperation. Since the college student respondents represent a proportion of the population with considerably greater than average future influence in occupational, political, and social positions, their attitudes and behaviors can have substantial future relevance to the future prospects of Mexican Americans and other minorities in the American social system.

Method of the study

Comparative Method

The interpretation of college student stereotypes of Mexican Americans, as for any ethnic group, can best be understood in a comparative context. It is not enough to know the positive or negative nature of the stereotypical character imagery. The social meaning of such ethnic imagery includes the need to consider stability and changes in ethnic imagery over time and between ethnic groups. Data reported here take into account this comparative perspective by including results for Mexican Americans in samples drawn in 1968 and again in 1982, as well as selected comparative ethnic imagery of Anglo Americans generally and of Blacks as another major minority status ethnic group.

The questionnaire instrument employed was an extension of that developed initially for the Katz and Braly (1933) stereotyping study of undergraduate students at Princeton University in 1932 and re-employed by Gilbert (1951) in 1950, and by Karlins, Coffman, and Walters (1969) in 1967. The questionnaire included 84 traits of varying positive, neutral, or negative cultural connotations. Each student respondent was asked to identify the traits he or she associated with each of ten listed racial and ethnic groups. The ethnic groups were Americans (generally), Blacks, Chinese, English, Germans, Irish, Italians, Japanese, Jews, and and Turks. The extension of the questionnaire began in random undergraduate sampling at Arizona State University in 1969 (Gordon & Hudson, 1970) with the addition of two ethnic groups--American Indians and Mexican Americans. The baseline data developed in 1969 for the latter two ethnic groups was continued for comparative purposes in another probability sample at Arizona State in 1982. In the reporting of results (Tables 1 and 2), the student selections are presented in terms of rank order (from highest selection [1] to lowest selection [10 or lower]) and in terms of the total percentage selecting a given trait.

Student Ethnic Composition

The Princeton students in the 1932 study were virtually all White, male, and Protestant. In the 1950 Princeton study there was more of a religious and ethnic mix, as a consequence of the post World War II G.I.Bill which supported veterans, allowing them to go to any college of their choice in which they could matriculate (Baltzel, 1964, pp. 341-342). The Arizona State University student ethnic mix in 1982 closely paralleled that of the Arizona State University mix in the 1969 study (Gordon, 1973). The ethnic mix breakdown in 1982 was 60% White Protestant, 29% Catholic, 6% Jewish, 2% Latter Day Saint, 2% Mexican American (generally Catholic), and 1% Black (generally Protestant). The ethnic diversity found at Arizona State in 1982, as in 1969, is a reflection of increased student diversity at colleges and universities generally (Crossland, 1971; Grant & Eiden, 1980), including Princeton where similar sampling and results occurred in 1967 (Karlins, Coffman, & Walters, 1969).

General Implications of the Sampling

It is argued here that the Princeton and Arizona State samples are generalizable to college students on the following grounds:

(1) There is evidence of the representativeness of college samples, including Katz's & Braly's (1933, p. 280) and Gilbert's (1951, p. 254) own arguments for the generality of their findings, and findings of the stability of similar results across different colleges and university samples (Guilford, 1931; Hartley, 1946; Hudson & Henze, 1969).

(2) Arizona and, hence, the state university, draws recent immigrants from other states (Inside Phoenix, 1985).

(3) The leading traits assigned to "Americans" generally were stable in all four studies spanning a half century--"intelligent," "industrious," and "materialistic" were the top three traits selected out of 84--while change was being registered in ethnic trait selections for Blacks, Jews, and other minority status groups.

(4) Independent samples drawn in a close time span at Arizona State University in 1969 and at Princeton University in 1967 produced the same basic pattern of faded hostile trait selections for minority status ethnic groups with markedly similar percentages and rank ordering (Gordon, 1973; Karlins, Coffman, & Walters, 1969).

Results and Implications

The student trait perceptions of Mexican Americans include a number of negative traits. With one exception the trait perceptions do not overlap with any traits perceived for Americans generally. As noted on Table 1, in both 1969 and 1982 the leading traits included "lazy," "ignorant," "unreliable," and "physically dirty." In this context the remaining highly ranked trait selections of "very religious," "loyal to family ties," "talkative," "quick-tempered," and "tradition-loving" presents a picture of a clannish ethnic group toward whom much social distance exists. For 1982 the one

Table 1

Stereotypes of American Generic Identity and of Mexican American Identity

	Americans (Generically)			
	1	2	3	4
	1932	1950	1969	1982
ait	% (Rank)	% (Rank)	% (Rank)	% (Rank)
lustrious	48 (1)	30 (3)	32 (3)	28 (3)
elligent	47 (2)	32 (2)	33 (2)	29 (1)
terialistic	33 (3)	37 (1)	44 (1)	33 (2)
bitious	33 (3)	21 (6)	17 (6)	12 (8)
ogressive	27 (5)	5 (10)	9	6
asure-Loving	26 (6)	27 (4)	18 (5)	10 (10)
ert	23 (7)	7 (9)	6	4
ficient	21 (8)	9 (7)	10 (9)	1
gressive	20 (9)	8 (8)	10 (9)	15 (6)
aight-Forward	19 (10)	1	1	1
actical	19 (10)	1	1	2
ortsmanlike	19 (10)	1	1	1
lividualistic	-	26 (5)	8	16 (4)
entifically-Minded	-	-	19 (4)	16 (4)
phisticated	-	-	10 (9)	13 (7)
aginative	-	-	16 (7)	12 (8)

			Mexican Americans	
			3	4
			1969	1982
ait			% (Rank)	% (Rank)
zy			25 (1)	20 (1)
ry Religious			20 (2)	14 (2)
asure-Loving			16 (3)	1
orant		13 (4)	12 (4)	
reliable			13 (4)	7 (6)
yal to Family Ties			12 (6)	13 (3)
ysically Dirty			11 (7)	9 (5)
kative			10 (8)	3 (8-9)
ick-Tempered			2 (9-10)	5 (7)
adition-Loving			2 (9-10)	3 (8-9)

Princeton University sample, n = 100. See Katz & Braly (1933).
Princeton University sample, n = 333. See Gilbert (1951).
Arizona State University sample, n - 459. See Gordon (1973).
Arizona State University sample, n = 139. See Gordon (1986)

Table 2

Changing Patterns of Negative Racial Identity Stereotypes

	Blacks			
	1	2	3	4
	1932	1950	1969	1982
Trait	% (Rank)	% (Rank)	% (Rank)	% (Rank)
Superstitious	84 (1)	42 (1)	10 (6)	9 (10)
Lazy	75 (2)	32 (3)	18 (2)	18 (1)
Happy-Go-Lucky	39 (3)	17 (6)	5	1
Ignorant	38 (4)	24 (4)	8 (9)	9 (10)
Musical	26 (5)	33 (2)	25 (1)	11 (5)
Ostentatious	26 (5)	11 (8)	14 (3)	10 (7)
Very Religious	24 (7)	17 (6)	5	1
Stupid	22 (8)	10 (9)	2	1
Physically Dirty	17 (9)	-	1	1
Naive	14 (10)	-	1	1
Sly	-	-	1	15 (2)
Aggressive	-	-	6	13 (3)
Intelligent	-	-	13 (4)	13 (3)
Loud	-	-	9 (8)	11 (5)
Materialistic	-	-	8 (9)	11 (5)
Arrogant	-	-	1	10 (7)
Sportsmanlike	-	-	6	9 (10)
Unreliable	-	-	10 (6)	6
Pleasure-Loving	-	19 (5)	12 (5)	4
Sensitive	-	-	1	4

1 Princeton University sample, n = 100. See Katz & Braly (1933).
2 Princeton University sample, n = 333. See Gilbert (1951).
3 Arizona State University sample, n = 459. See Gordon (1973).
4 Arizona State University sample, n = 139. See Gordon (1986)

trait found to be overlapping with Americans generally--that of "pleasure loving"--had declined from from 16% to 1%.

As can be seen on Table 2, which shows student trait perceptions of Blacks, the ethnic imagery of Mexican Americans is more negative as a whole than that of Blacks. For Blacks such negative trait perceptions by the time of the 1982 study of "superstitious," "lazy," and "sly" are joined by such positive cultural traits as "sportsmanlike" and "intelligent." This is not surprising in a Southwestern state locale like Arizona for reasons noted below.

Conclusions and Implications

It is well documented that indigenous minority groups tend to elicit more aggressive hostility from dominant ethnic groups than do migrant minorities (Lieberson, 1961; Price, 1950). Blacks in contemporary social terms would be indigenous to the American South but migrants to the Southwest. As such, ethnic antipathy toward the more indigenous Mexican Americans in the Southwest is deeply rooted in their historical experience. The negative ethnic perceptions of a substantial student body minority of 5% (for their "quick-tempered" perception of Mexican Americans) to 20% (for "lazy") is a reflection of the troubled Mexican American past experience.

The historical ethnic hostility generated in the forced transfer from Mexican to American citizenship following the Mexican-American War and Treaty of Guadalupe Hidalgo in 1848 continued for generations (McWilliams, 1949). In more contemporary terms there have been continuing intergroup conflicts. The zoot-suit Mexican-Anglo Los Angeles riots in the 1940s (Turner & Surace, 1956), the Mexican American rioting in Phoenix in the 1960s (*Report of the National Advisory Commission on Civil Disorders*, 1968, pp. 117; 165), and the conflicts generated by hundreds of thousands of illegal Mexican immigrants each year since the 1970s along with ongoing assimilation problems (Alvarez, 1973; Lopez, 1976) are symptomatic of continuing mutual ethnic distrust between Mexican and Anglo Americans.

Alvarez (1973), Lopez (1976), and other analysts have noted that Mexican Americans have responded to negative or indifferent ethnic imagery toward them by a growing sense of ethnic pride and sociopolitical cohesion. Such cohesion has been reinforced to address a number of social problems facing Mexican Americans. Within Arizona and nationally,

Mexican Americans continue to experience substantial housing segregation (James, McCummings, & Tynan, 1984, p. 51), lower quality housing at every per capita income level (Gordon & Mayer, 1985), and often continued exclusion from equal educational and employment opportunities (Simpson & Yinger, 1985, pp. 187-189; 342-346).

In this context, there is an historical relationship between ethnic hostility and intergroup conflict during times of social stress. A classic example is the manner in which the negative ethnic imagery of Japanese ethnicity resulted in manifestly loyal Japanese American citizens being rounded up and placed in detention camps for much of World War II (Bloom and Riemer, 1949). The ongoing effects on contemporary Japanese American identity is still evident (Woodrum, 1981). However, that kind of dominant Anglo American societal reaction came during a period when negative ethnic imagery was at much higher levels than is evident in more recent findings. College students in the first studies in the 1930s lived in a much more homogeneous higher education collegiate environment as well as in a less urbanized pluralistic society which had not yet become globally involved in affairs of a racially and ethnically diverse world society.

While in the most recent study a substantial minority of up to 20% of college students expressed hostile perceptions toward Mexican Americans, this proportion is much lower than that shown in documented studies of earlier student generations. We do not have systematic stereotyping data from the 1930s through the 1950s for Mexican Americans as we do for Blacks and a number of other ethnic groups. However, to gain a sense of this generational difference, note on Table 2 the sharp, statistically significant declines in hostile stereotypes of Blacks. The substantial majorities of 84% and 75% who perceived of Blacks as "superstitious" and "lazy" in 1932 had declined to 9% and 18% by 1982. These hostile perceptions remained in the top ten of those selected but the sharp reduction by 1982 in hostile perceptions of Blacks appears to parallel the similar levels of the most recent study involving perceptions of Mexican Americans.

The straight line significant decline in negative ethnic stereotyping of minority status groups between the 1930s and 1960s gave rise to hopes of a permanent long term shift toward mutual ethnic pluralistic respect (e.g. Bogardus, 1968; Karlins, Coffman, & Walters, 1969). The reemergence at lower levels of hostile stereotypes, including those evident toward Mexican Americans, has given rise to new concerns. Some analysts hold that instead of a long term shift, the low levels of expressed ethnic hostility in the 1960s was a secular trend. In this perspective it is argued that the high positive acceptance of ethnic pluralism two decades ago was a consequence of unusual situational experiences relating to the social conditions during and following World War II which gave rise to the civil rights movement and reforms of that period (Carlsson & Karlsson, 1970; Duncan, 1982). In this respect, it is of interest that the more ethnically accepting young adult 1960s age cohort, now in their forties, gave substantially more voting support to the 1984 presidential candidacy of Walter Mondale than did the young 1980s cohort itself (*USA Today* Poll, 1984).

However, despite these concerns, the overall 1982 results appear to substantiate the continuing decline generally in negative ethnic stereotyping. Over three-quarters of the students did not accept any negative perception trait respecting Mexican Americans. As such there is support for the prospect that pluralistic accommodation among Anglos, Mexican Americans, and others continues to be the predominant attitude.

While this overall positive and accepting pattern exists, the minority of students who hold hostile perceptions of Mexican Americans, as well as toward Blacks and other minority status group members, appear to hold their views more strongly (Gordon, 1991). A consequence has been the emergence on American college campuses of increased open conflict of an interpersonal and intergroup nature. Symptomatic of this emergence is the finding of Howard Ehrlich, Director of the National Institute Against Prejudice and Violence, who reported that between 1986 and 1989 there were 175 racial conflict incidents at American universities (Magner, 1989). When a racial riot broke out at Arizona State University in the spring of 1989, as one of those reported by Ehrlich, news of the events was covered on the front page of the *New York Times* with coverage of serious incidents as well at the Universities of Michigan, Stanford, and Wisconsin.

The major news coverage concern was reflective of how increasingly important college level education has become to the futures of most individuals across racial and ethnic lines. As such, the universities are no longer, if they ever were, cloistered halls of ivy. Instead, they will clearly be a center focus of public attention in terms of racial and ethnic relations, including those between Mexican Americans and all others in the society.

The Mexican American population in Arizona and nationally, and Hispanics more generally, constitute the most rapidly growing ethnic population in the United States (James, McCummings, & Tynan, 1984, p.

5). Conservative projections from U.S. census data indicate that in the 21st century between one-fifth and one-quarter of all Americans will be Hispanic, mostly of Mexican American ethnicity.

Their size, rapid growth, and relative concentration in the Southwest has positioned Mexican Americans to challenge others politically and economically to achieve equality of treatment and opportunity. The migrant labor protest movement of recent decades, led by Cesar Chavez, is symptomatic that the challenge is being taken up within the Mexican American community (Mathiessen, 1970). While that protest movement reinforced images of Mexican Americans as rural based, the current reality, evident in U.S. Census reports, is that over three-quarters of Mexican Americans are now urban based. As was the case with the Black community, the urban setting for minority status groups is more conducive to effective protest communication and organization than the rural setting. Consequently, it can be expected that unless both the imagery and practical behavior toward Mexican Americans becomes more accommodating than in the past, Mexican Americans will increasingly challenge politically and in other ways their inequitable position in American society.

The ethnic attitudes that college students, as well as others, hold will be one of the influences on the nature of any interethnic conflicts, conflict resolution, and accommodation processes that are likely to occur. The future attitudes and behavior of this generation of college students toward their Mexican American fellow citizens will constitute one of the major emergent tests of the American Creed of equality of treatment and opportunity. Given the size and growth of the Mexican American population, the outcome will affect the entire social, educational, economic, and political life of American society. The test of genuinely accepting attitudes will go beyond stereotypical imagery studies. It will involve public and private policies and behaviors which enable Mexican Americans to close the still wide gaps between them and most other Americans in such basic areas of social life as educational and occupational opportunities as well as the cost and quality of housing and health care.

References

Alvarez, R. (1973). The psycho-historical and socioeconomic development of the Chicano community in the United States. Social Science Quarterly, 14, 920-942.
Baltzel, D. (1964). The Protestant establishment. New York: Random House.
Bloom, L. & Reimer, R. (1949). Removal and return. Berkeley: University of California Press.
Blumer, H. (1969). Symbolic interactionism: Perspective and method. Englewood Cliffs, NJ: Prentice-Hall.
Bogardus, E. S. (1968). Comparing racial distance in Ethiopia, South Africa, and the United States. Sociology and Social Research, 52, 149-156.
Carlsson, B. & Karlsson, K. (1970). Age, cohorts and the generation of generations. American Sociological Review, 35, 710-718.
Crossland, G. E. (1971). Minority access to college. New York: Schoken.
Duncan, O. D. (1982). Recent cohorts lead reflection of sex typing. Sex Roles, 8, 127-133.
Gilbert, G. M. (1951). Stereotype persistence and change among college students. Journal of Abnormal and Social Psychology, 46, 245-254.
Glazer, N. & Moynihan, D. P. (1963). Beyond the melting pot: The Negroes, Puerto Ricans, Jews, Italians, and Irish of New York City. Cambridge: M.I.T. and Harvard University Press.
Gordon, L. (1991). Race relations in higher education: The case of Arizona State University. In P. Altbach and K. Lomotey (Eds.), The racial crisis in higher education. Buffalo: State University of New York Press.
Gordon, L. (1986). College student stereotypes of Blacks and Jews on two campuses: Four studies spanning 50 years. Sociology and Social Research, 70, 201-202.
Gordon, L. (1973). The fragmentization of literary stereotypes of Jews and Negroes among college students. Pacific Sociological Review, 16, 411-425.
Gordon, L. & Hudson, J. W. (1970). Emergent white Protestant student perception of Jews. Journal for the Scientific Study of Religion, 9, 235-238.
Gordon, L. & Mayer, A. J. (1985). The cost and quality of housing by income level of Anglos, Blacks, and Hispanics: Phoenix 1980. A Report for the Phoenix Equal Opportunity Department and the U.S. Department of Housing and Urban Development.
Grant, W. V. & Eiden, L. N. (1980). Digest of education statistics. Washington, D.C.: National Center for Education Statistics.
Guilford, J. P. (1931). Racial preferences of a thousand American university students. Journal of Social Psychology, 2, 179-204.
Hartley, E. (1946). Problems in prejudice. New York: King's Crown.
Hudson, J. W. & Henze, L. (1969). Campus values in mate selection: a replication. Journal of Marriage and the Family, 31, 772-777.
Inside Phoenix. (1985). Phoenix Newspapers, Incorporated, Annual Publication.
James, F. J., McCummings, B. I., & Tynan, E. A. (1984). Minorities in the sunbelt. New Brunswick, NJ: Center for Urban Policy Research.
Karlins, M., Coffman, T. L., & Walters, G. (1969). On the fading of social stereotypes:

Studies in three generations of college students. *Journal of Personality and Social Psychology*, 13, 1-16.

Katz, D. & Braly, K. W. (1933). Racial stereotypes of 100 college students. *Journal of Abnormal and Social Psychology*, 28, 280-290.

Lieberson, S. (1961). Societal theory of race and ethnic relations. *American Sociological Review*, 26, 902-910.

Lopez, D. E. (1976). The social consequences of Chicano home/school bilingualism. *Social Problems*, 24, 234-246.

Magner, D. K. (1989). Blacks and whites on the campuses: Behind the ugly racist incidents, student isolation and insensitivity. *The Chronicle of Higher Education*, XXXV, (April 26), A28-A32.

Mathiessen, P. (1970). *Sal si puedes: Cesar Chavez and the new revolution.* New York: Random House.

Martinelli, P. C. (1989). *Ethnicity in the sunbelt: Italian American migrants in Scottsdale, Arizona.* New York: AMS Press.

McWilliams, C. (1949). *North from Mexico.* Philadelphia: J. B. Lippencott.

Price, A. G. (1950). *White settlers and native peoples.* Melbourne: Georgian House.

Report of the National Advisory Commission on Civil Disorders (1968). New York: Bantam.

Rosenthal, P. & Jacobson, L. (1968). *Pygmalion in the classroom.* New York: Holt, Rinehart and Winston.

Simpson, G. E. & Yinger, J. M. (1985). *Racial and cultural minorities: An analysis of prejudice and discrimination* (5th edition). New York: Plenum.

Thomas, W. I. (1931). The relation of research to the social process in *Essays on research in the social sciences*. Washington, D.C.: The Brookings Institution, 189.

Turner, R. H. & Surace, S. J. (1956). Zoot-suiters and Mexicans: Symbols in crowd behavior. *American Journal of Sociology*, 62, 14-20.

USA Today Poll (November 5, 1984). It's Reagan in nearly every category, 1.

Woodrum, E. (1981). An assessment of Japanese-American assimilation, pluralism, and subordination. *American Journal of Sociology*, 87, 157-169.

Chapter IX

Bernal and Martinelli

Ethnic Identity Research and Policy Implications for Mexican Americans

by

John A. García
University of Arizona

The persistence of ethnic identification and the dynamic nature of salient factors that contribute to its vitality has been the subject of continuous inquiry for social and behavioral scientists. The foci of this chapter are: 1) to discuss some important dimensions and issues affecting conceptions and measurement of ethnic identity; and 2) to relate the persistence of ethnic identification in public policy and participation. Clearly, both maintenance and the changing forms of ethnic identification are found within the Mexican origin community in the United States. The basis for such a sense of communality is influenced by interpersonal relationships between the individual, the group, and sociopolitical institutions. In order to explore these important relationships with Mexican American identity, this chapter is divided into four sections. They are: the role of ethnicity in a complex, modern society; the dimensions and functions served by ethnic identity; research directions and identity; and the linkages between ethnic identity and participation in public policy arenas.

Role of Ethnicity in Modern Society

One possible perspective in the discussion of ethnic identification for those of Mexican origin in the 1980's is that of a historical artifact that bears little relation to their day-to-day living, values, and behaviors. Many discussions of modernization usually identify as one of its casualties the decline of ethnicity. As primordial interests extend beyond kinship and tribal, other social networks and relationships develop (i.e., occupational, class, secondary associations, etc.) (Nielsen, 1985). As societies become more modern, this pattern can be characterized as "diffusion-erasure" in which social roles and relations extend beyond primary family ties and previous national origin (Clark, Kaufman, and Pierce, 1976).

Accompanying modernization is industrialization, in which economic structures and relationships evolve from traditional agricultural and bartering economies to large-scale manufactured goods and mechanized production (Nielsen, 1985). The changes to greater mechanization and skilled labor requirements also contribute to the erosion of ethnicity and kinship networks. In addition, political modernization includes greater decentralization of political institutions and more points of access for groups and individuals. The latter dimension reflects the process of nation building in which the integration process includes a common sense of citizenship, affective allegiance and loyalty, a core set of societal values, and multiple social identities (Ross, 1982).

We have described a process for which the pressures of assimilation and acculturation operate on the adaptive experiences of immigrant and minority populations. Eventually, acceptance by the host society and feelings of membership by the immigrant/minority person occurs (Portes, Parker, and Cobas, 1980). Yet results of the modernization and industrialization process in the United States have indicated some other outcomes that impact on ethnicity. Economic competition based on ethnicity, peripheral social and economic location and exploitation, structural differentiation, cultural division of labor, and social, economic, and cultural boundaries are found in this modern society (Portes & Mozo, 1985).

For example, conflict theories suggest that cultural preparedness and/or similarities of immigrant and minority members with the "host society" will enable them to enjoy greater upward mobility. In addition, greater knowledge about the society and greater achievement, economically and educationally, become more common (Portes et al., 1980). With modernity, people experience greater occupational, economic, and educational differentiation from their ethnic cohorts. One factor that influences the degree of immersion with the dominant society lies with the person's perceptions and experiences, particularly those regarding discriminatory interactions. The source of conflict occurs when the culturally prepared and upwardly mobile immigrant/minority member develops a better understanding of the functions of social groups in American society (Portes, 1984). If that understanding indicates some differential, negative treatment, then the immigrant/minority person can develop a critical consciousness of institutions and policies because they suggest non-acceptance by the dominant society. This critical consciousness will be grounded in national origin ethnicity (Portes & Truelove, 1987).

A number of other approaches or theories reflect this theme of structural relationships within American society that serve to reinforce the persistence of ethnicity. One such approach deals with the direct effects of demographic, economic, and social structures on the persistence of ethnicity. For example, issues of economic well-being, labor market participation, and concentration in residential area in urban areas, and political representation can delineate societal differentiation based on ethnicity. The latter example (i.e., political representation) moves us to another theoretical perspective which can be characterized as political incorporation. In this case, the effects of ethnic persistence on the polity results in governmental adjustments to accommodate ethnic divisions (Esman, 1985). Examples of political incorporation would include specialized programs to serve particular groups or affirmative action activities. Developmentally, the political construction of ethnicity could follow political incorporation. That is, recognition of ethnicity serves as the legitimate basis for political reorganization by the central government. Such recognition acknowledges prior divisions, increases ethnic identification, and allows for new mobilization for formerly unrecognized groups (Nielsen, 1985).

One final model that warrants some discussion is referred to as the community theses of ethnic/racial mobilization. In this perspective, a sense of community is designated by ethnic/racial boundaries, and it is placed in a subordinate position (Huckfeldt, 1983). External influences define power and economic relations, while the meaning attributed to ethnicity is defined by internal and external interpretations. The internal pressures for redefinition by the ethnic community result in the development of positive reformulation of their ethnic experiences and pursuit of collective activities. For the community theses the sociopolitical participation of group members is based upon the presence of a salient sense of ethnic consciousness.

This discussion of the persistence of ethnicity in the face of the forces of modernization and industrialization incorporates numerous common themes. They include: structural relations that are defined, in part or exclusively, by ethnic/racial boundaries; social relations and networks that reinforce a sense of group membership; cognitive, affective, and evaluative dimensions of a sense of ethnicity; the relative ease by which a group can coalesce based on ethnicity rather than some other social category; and the presence of subordinate-dominant relations. A key ingredient in this discussion is the interactive nature of the persistence of ethnic identification. Yet our purpose is not only to present an analytical discussion examining the existence of ethnic identification, but to answer the question--"why does it exist in its multifaceted aspects?"

Dimensions and Functions of Ethnicity

The other chapters on the issue of ethnic identity among the Mexican origin community in the United States further substantiate its persistence and multidimensionality. Part of the effort to examine ethnic identity entails the designation of the boundaries which contain the many aspects of ethnicity. The factors of national origin, language, culture, residential concentration, familialism, and similar phenotypical characteristics serve as contributors to ethnicity (García, 1979). Besides the definition of what those boundaries might be the degree of ethnic awareness among members who exhibit "ethnic" characteristics represents the psychological aspect of ethnicity.

The concept of social identity represents a cognitive dimension of one's self in relation to a variety of social categories and roles (Arce, 1981). Clearly, Mexican Americans may define themselves in terms of gender, class, occupation, national origin, and religious and familial roles. The relevance of ethnic identification rests in the centrality of that identity within the individual. One's cognitive map will be influenced by interactions with other persons, institutions and their representatives, and formal and informal structures that affect life chances and opportunities.

Certainly the perception of the commonalities that define one as Mexican American has been a central focus of research on ethnic identity. It is quite evident that research on ethnic identity is a dynamic process in which components may change over time and to which situational factors make a contribution. It is a multidimensional concept and Mexican Americans live within a constellation of social identities. Work by Keefe and Padilla (1987) represents a significant effort to develop the multidimensional concept of ethnicity, as well as operational measures of dimensions of Chicano "ethnicity". Their research suggests that cultural awareness and ethnic identity are two major dimensions that, in combination, produce a variety of manifestations of ethnicity.

More specifically, some of the more important factors related to ethnic identity include: language (use, proficiency, loyalty); preferences for particular foods and music; knowledge and participation in cultural traditions; value and belief systems; ethnic awareness and pride; associational preferences to interact with other Mexican Americans; behavior in conformance with ethnic values, beliefs; conformance with ethnic values, beliefs, and orientations; and historical knowledge of the Mexican American community and its origin. Generational distance from Mexico and barrio residence also serve as key components of Mexican American identity (Keefe and Padilla, 1987). The other factor related to ethnic identity is that of self-identification. Clearly, measures of ethnic identity incorporate both socio-psychological and behavioral components (García, 1979).

One of the empirical questions facing researchers is how identifiable are ethnic behaviors. A number of research issues and questions still remain for the examination of Mexican American identity. Among those items, the development of the operationalization of ethnic identity will be influenced by the dynamic nature of the social phenomenon. Is ethnic identity a long-term social identity or a transitory situation? What is the extent of the variations of ethnic identity, and how do these variations affect standardized measures? What are the manifest and latent functions of ethnic identity? What are the psychological and symbolic functions of ethnic identity for the individual as well as the group?

Research Directions and Identity

Incorporation of gender identity. While questions have been raised regarding research issues in ethnic identity, there are a number of specific suggestions that can encourage the expansion of research on ethnic identity or give it new directions. The first area involves the needed incorporation of gender identity into the examination of Mexican American identity. What are the effects of the presence of gender identity among Mexican American women's identity and behavior (Baca-Zinn, 1980)? Given the potential centrality of these two identities, are there specific attitudes (i.e., efficacy, trust, self-esteem, etc.) and behaviors influenced by one or the other identity, or does the interaction of the two social identities create an independent effect? If the effects differ given situational factors, socialization patterns, and structural relations, then this might suggest that individuals have options they can pursue; and this would provide useful insights into the process of ethnic identity and its manifestations. An understanding of gender identity and its influences on ethnicity is an important area of expansion.

Latino identity. The second area of research that warrants greater attention is that of a concomitant identity --Latino or Hispanic identity. The persistence of an ethnic identity is, in part, due to its being a social construct which can have a purposive function. The terms, Latino or Hispanic, are now widely used in social and policy settings. One can look at Latino identity (Padilla, 1985) as a structural type of identification which transcends national origin boundaries. The use of such identity serves the purposes of mobilizing for social action and expanding the parameters of group membership. Padilla's (1985) work on Latino consciousness discusses this form of identity as a strategic choice in which political capital can be enhanced with potentially greater numbers and resources.

On the other hand, other researchers have examined the evidence for Latino identity and the "reality of this social construct." Melville (1988) recognizes the common usage of Hispanic, but argues its inappropriateness since it does not recognize the Amerindian and African components for these populations. Similarly, Nelson and Tienda (1985) suggest that the Hispanic category conceals national origin complexities and still relatively isolated and distinct ethnic communities. Finally, Portes and Truelove (1987) conclude that the label "Hispanic" is problematic because of the diversity of the groups included. Yet there are some trends to imply convergence in political orientations and voting.

Research on Latino identity centers around issues of multiple ethnic identities, the extent to which Mexican Americans incorporate this social identity, contributing factors that comprise a Latino identity, the utility of such an identity, and the salience of Latino identity. While the public use of the terms Hispanic and Latino continue to expand, researchers know very little about the dynamics, persistence, and relevance of Latino identity for Mexican Americans. Demographically, the extent of exogamy among different Hispanic groups has increased, so that the "reality" of a Latino identity may reflect partially the greater contact among specific Hispanic groups.

Mexican American Identity

Intergenerational transmission of ethnic identity. Despite the characterization as an immigrant population, many Mexican Americans have been in the United States for many generations. Therefore, an area of intergenerational transmission of ethnicity and identity is another important area of research. As previously stated, the dynamic nature of ethnicity may result in transmission of ethnic identity, yet its manifestation can be very different from one generation to another (Rogler, Santana-Cooney, and Ortiz, 1980). For example, language is viewed as a central dimension of ethnic identity. The persistence of Spanish language with younger generations is less prevalent, so that ethnic identity may include for them Spanish language loyalty and not its usage. How and what kinds of ethnic cues, symbols, and experiences are conveyed from one generation to another is not a process that is well understood. Certainly language theories and theories of cognitive development can serve to identify the process, with the psychological concept of self as the domain in which ethnic identity is incorporated. Unfortunately, the attention on the transmission of ethnic identity, when researched, is limited to the young and adolescents. One would assume that the persistence and functions of ethnic identity do not end with early maturation process.

Recent work by Bernal, Knight, Garza, Ocampo, & Cota (1990) attempts to explore aspects of cognitive social learning, cognitive development, and self-esteem systems within a theoretical framework examining ethnic identity among Mexican American children. Their work on 6 to 10 year-olds and preschool children includes methodological refinements for these age groups, as well as testing of developmental changes. Clearly, ethnic identity involves social learning and cognitive development.

In a sense the previously identified areas of research are an attempt to expand the the constellation of social identities that seem to be intertwined with that of ethnic identity. In addition, the call for longitudinal and intergenerational studies is an attempt to understand the changes occurring within the Mexican American community and their ethnic identity. While specific factors have been identified as contributors to ethnic identity, one can examine the "mediating" factors that facilitate or impede ethnic identity. Such factors would include: age at immigration (for the foreign-born); educational attainment; ethnic composition of the neighborhood; the neighborhood; family cohesion; the density, nature, and types of social networks (i.e., voluntary interactions with persons that can influence values, attitudes, and behavior); gender; structural milieu (i.e., opportunity structure, presence or absence of discrimination, etc.); and occupational status.

For example, a Mexican American who resides in a homogeneous "Mexican" neighborhood can heighten his/her cultural behaviors and values by regular interaction with other Mexican Americans (neighbors and/or family members). Hurtado and Arce (1986) argue that the impact of language and nativity must be considered when attempting to define the heterogeneity of the Mexican origin community. They indicate significant differences are evident in how sub-groups label themselves in a variety of settings.

While there may be ethnic contexts for occupation, neighborhood composition, and other identified mediating factors, most of these variables do not make up the core of ethnic identity. Methodologically, one would expect these variables to have indirect effects on the presence and nature of ethnic identity, while the cultural dimensions "provide" the direct contributions to ethnic identity. Thus the research agenda should include more attention directed to the theoretical formulation of mediating factors in an overall model of ethnic identity.

This brief discussion of some of the major dimensions of research on ethnic identity, as well as needed areas of more intensive research, reinforce our position that the concept of ethnic identity is both multidimensional and very complex. Clearly, the psychological dimension of ethnicity is most critical; and this dimension will influence how some behavioral manifestations and collective pursuits and outcomes result. One of the tasks of this chapter is to make some linkages of ethnic identity to public policy arenas. The final section of this chapter relates this phenomenon to public participation in policy arenas. In other words, "What is the role of ethnic identity in the mobilization of the Mexican American community for directed purposes?"

Ethnic Identity and Public Policy Participation

The previous discussion of ethnic identity has tried to establish themes of group membership, boundaries of social identity, and a sense of ethnic solidarity related to ethnic identity. In this manner, ethnic identity works to define common goals, claims for membership, and the ideological basis for mobilization of the members. Therefore, the discussion of mobilization focuses on the means to facilitate the expression of group solidarity or ethnic identity (Nielsen, 1985, 140-141). From this perspective, the presence of components of ethnic identity serve as the catalysts for group mobilization.

Mexican American Identity

Mobilization refers to the allocation of some of the group members' resources, a psychological commitment to the group, and the "physical" courage to engage in collective efforts. Certainly the constellation of social identities that an individual may possess can be overlapping, nested, and/or cross-cutting. One can view ethnic identity as a latent dimension of self which can be converted to a more active state as a result of the mobilization process. Drawing upon the work of Nielsen (1985) on minority group participation, we would like to present some critical factors that contribute to the facilitation of group solidarity or ethnic identity. In a sense, we are establishing a link in which the capacity for participation of an ethnically identifiable group, Mexican Americans, is developed. Six sets of factors can increase Mexican Americans' capacity to engage in collective pursuits in various policy arenas. The factors are: 1) size of the latent group; 2) resources of the group; 3) the potential supply of leaders; 4) homogeneity of interests; 5) potential control of events; and 6) organizational potential (Nielsen, 1985, 143-145).

Group size. For Mexican Americans, the issues of group membership and population growth have focused on their growing presence in the United States. If our earlier discussion of the emergence of a Latino "ethnic" identity is relevant, then the size of this group has increased significantly. At the same time, sheer numbers do not automatically translate into major mobilization efforts or immediate policy changes. Clearly the 1980's is the decade that Hispanics began with high expectations that a growing population would insure more effective political participation. Yet major changes for the well-being of Mexican Americans and other Latinos have been very uneven so far. Obviously, the issue of size of the Mexican American community can increase the capacity to participate with a greater visibility, resource base, and response to mobilization efforts.

The resources of the group. The second factor follows from the size consideration, as the resources within the Mexican American community can afford greater effectiveness to facilitate Mexican American policy expressions. The range of resources that can be used in mobilization efforts would include: surplus incomes (or resources) for organizational support; a growing middle class; entrepreneurial segments in the community; expertise like legal and financial knowledge; and a large voting constituency.

Within the framework of American public policy, resources would include an economic base and "slack monetary supplies" to direct the specific policy arenas to either demarcate or influence policy formulation, adoption, and implementation favorable to the groups' interests and needs. In addition to economic resources, social status, expertise, and networks, residential concentration and organizational bases serve as important resources to facilitate the expression of ethnic solidarity. Certainly the intensity and persuasiveness of ethnic identity can serve as a catalyst for resource building within the Mexican American community.

Potential leadership pool. The third factor refers to the potential leadership pool available for mobilization. Our discussion of mobilization centers around the pursuit of collective goods and goals. The leadership pool for the Mexican American community would come from individuals who are not committed to the obtainment of collective goods for other social groups (Nielsen, 1985, 142-144). In a sense, a society that segments portions of its population (economically, racially, ethnically, etc.) creates some outlets for leadership through ethnic group boundaries. That is, opportunities to exercise leadership can be met by individuals who are not afforded opportunities in other groups; and/or they are committed to collective interests of the Mexican American community. In any event, the potential pool of leaders represents the activation and conversion of ethnic identity into a collective mode.

Organizational dimensions of mobilization. The fourth set of factors in the mobilization process deals with the organizational dimensions of mobilization. Also, with the selection of issues and policy arenas to engage in agenda setting and influencing activities. The first aspect can be described as the potential for control of events. Mobilization serving to maintain a sense of ethnic identity has been discussed previously. This factor interjects an evaluative dimension as the "appropriateness" of mobilizing around a given issue. Some considerations include: available resources; saliency of the issue to the group; probability of resolution of the issue; and definable parameters of power and authority.

Consensus of within-group interests. The fifth factor interacts with the advisability of entering certain policy arenas and issues. It can be referred to as the consensus of interests within the Mexican American community. Not only do the events and issues have to be identified as important, but the outcomes have to show effects on the community in very similar ways. The latter point is important since it represents the homogeneity of both interests and impact on Mexican Americans. This degree of universality increases the capacity for participation as a cohesive community.

Organizational potential of the community. Finally, the sixth factor is described as the organizational potential of the Mexican American community. Characteristics of organizational potential deal with the ease of tapping of resources and community commitment for collective pursuits. The extent of geographic dispersion or concentration will affect organizational style, structure, and size. For example, the geographic concentration of Mexican Americans in urban neighborhoods or in rural communities can facilitate organizational development by establishing a territorial base, identifiable membership, and common experience.

An additional consideration for the organizational potential is the quality of communication among members of the Mexican American community. Not only does a common language (in terms of mother tongue or bilingualism) become quite relevant, but shared symbols and cues serve to enhance a cohesive organization. Finally, mobilization and its manifestations in an organizational mode are the result of social interactions. Thus, the density of networks within the Mexican American community affects the quality of communication and the ease of tapping resources. While our comments have been centered around the mobilization of the Mexican American community, the "internal" considerations of solidarity and collective participation serve as important prerequisites for effective participation in policy arenas. Thus, our discussion of the persistence of ethnic identity and policy implications is really an analysis of the persistence of identity, its multidimensional nature, and its nature in facilitating the expression of group solidarity.

Identity and Public Policy: A Key Linkage

Our discussion of ethnic identity suggests that its persistence is the result of common experiences among Mexican origin persons and structural relations that establish some "ethnic" boundaries. The dynamic nature of ethnic identity and its sociopsychological roots is characterized by identifiable boundaries of the Mexican American experience. Feelings of solidarity and commonalties serve as the internal link in a chain of factors that enhance the capacity for Mexican Americans to participate in policymaking arenas. What serve as anchors of ethnic identity provide the psychological base for defining community and creating a resource base (Dashefsky, 1975). Our discussion of the research issues is intended to provide better insight into the bases of ethnic identity, and the functions it can serve.

Subsequently, the persistence of ethnic identity helps to define group goals, ideological perspectives, and a framework of analysis to evaluate the location of the Mexican American community in relation to the existing social structures, and establish a policy agenda with strong support from the community. Our list of contributing factors to improve the capacity for effective participation attempts to identify links in a chain of collective interests and pursuits. The symbols used in mobilization, motivations tapped for involvement, and anticipated rewards derived from participation are partly grounded in the manifestations of ethnic identity. While we do not identify the specific issue areas or policy agenda nor the kinds of influences Mexican Americans can have on policy outcomes, the underlying premise is that identity plays a key role in mobilizing this community. Specific issue areas of concern and interest include educational programs and resource allocation, job training and development, political empowerment and the like. Effective mobilization can affect the shaping of how the issues are defined, policy recommendations are formulated, and success in adopting favorable policies. Hopefully, this discussion will help to integrate the concept of ethnic identity into the mobilzation process and participation in policymaking arenas.

References

Arce, C. H. (1981). A reconsideration of Chicano culture and identity. Daedulus, 110, 177-91.
Baca-Zinn, M. (1980). Gender and ethnic identity among Chicanas. Frontiers, 5, 18-24.
Bernal, M. E., Knight, G. P., Garza, C. A., Ocampo K. A., and Cota, M. K. (1990). The development of ethnic identity in Mexican American children. Hispanic Journal of Behavioral Sciences, 12, 3-24.
Clark, M., Kaufman, S., & Pierce, R. (1976). Exploration of acculturation: Toward a model of ethnic identity. Human Organization, 35, 231-238.
Dashefsky, A. (1975). Theoretical frameworks in the study of ethnic identity: Toward a social psychology of ethnicity. Ethnicity, 2, 10-18.
Esman, M. (1985). Two dimensions of ethnic politics: A defense of homeland and immigrant rights. Ethnic and Racial Studies, 8, 428-440.
García, M. (1979). Development of a Cuban identity questionnaire. Hispanic Journal of Behavioral Sciences, 1, 247-261.
Huckfeldt, R. (1983). Social contexts of ethnic politics: Ethnic loyalties, political loyalties, and social support. American Politics Quarterly, 11, 91-123.
Hurtado, A. and C. Arce (1986). Mexicans, Chicanos, Mexican Americans, or Pochos: The impact of language and nativity on ethnic labelling. Aztlan, 17, 103-130.
Keefe, S. and Padilla, A. (1987). Chicano ethnicity. Albuquerque: University of New Mexico Press.
Melville, M. (1988). "Hispanics: Race, class or ethnicity?" The Journal of Ethnic Studies, 16, 67-83.
Nelson, C. & Tienda, M. (1985). The structure of Hispanic ethnicity: Historical and contemporary perspectives. Ethnic and Racial Studies, 8, 49-73.
Nielsen, F. (1985). Toward a theory of ethnic solidarity in modern societies. American Sociological Review, 50, 133-149.
Padilla, F. (1985). On the nature of Latino ethnicity. Social Science Quarterly, 66, 651-664.
Portes, A. (1984). The rise of ethnicity: Determinants of ethnic perceptions among Cuban exiles in Miami. American Sociological Review, 49, 383-397.
Portes, A. & Mozo, R. (1985). Political adaptation process of Cubans and other ethnic minorities in the U.S.: A preliminary analysis. International Migration Review, 19, 35-63.
Portes, A., Parker, R., & Cobas, J. (1980). Assimilation or consciousness: Perceptions of U.S. society among recent immigrants to the U.S. Social Forces, 59, 200-224.
Portes, A. and Truelove, C. (1987). Making sense out of diversity: Recent research on Hispanic minorities in the United States. Annual Review of Sociology, 13, 359-385.
Rogler, L., Santana-Cooney, R., & Ortiz, V. (1980). Intergenerational change in ethnic identity in Puerto Rican families. International Migration Review, 14, 193-215.
Ross, J. (1982). Urban development and the politics of ethnicity: A conceptual approach. Ethnic and Racial Studies, 5, 440-456.

Mexican American Identity

Chapter X

Bernal and Martinelli

Theoretical Conceptualizations, Definitions, and Measurement of Ethnic Identity

by

Martha E. Bernal
Arizona State University

In her introductory chapter to this book, Phylis Martinelli has described the different ways in which ethnic identity has been conceptualized in the literature. Based on this review, she has identified two central themes that cut across all the chapters in this book. One theme is the symbolic interaction approach to the understanding of ethnic identity. This theme is either implied or directly expressed in the chapters. It emphasizes the relationship between the individual's psychological self and the ethnic group. The second theme is the relation between the ethnic group and the core or dominant group. Within these two themes, ethnic identity is a result of both intra and intergroup processes, and these processes involve the use of symbols such as language, cultural norms, values, and preferences. The formation of ethnic identity, whether it be in young children just learning about their ethnic selves or adults reformulating their ethnic identity, involves the processes of enculturation or ethnic socialization within the ethnic family and community, as well as acculturation or adaptation to the core society. It requires sensitivity to the information about ethnicity and ethnic group membership that is communicated by significant own-group others, and is subject to the evaluations of the core society.

Goals of This Chapter

It is the author's task in this concluding chapter to examine, compare, and contrast the theoretical conceptualizations and definitions of ethnic identity in the different chapters, and to relate them, when appropriate, to the measurement of ethnic identity. To facilitate this task, it is useful to provide an outline that orders the different kinds of variables which have been implicated in the above analysis of ethnic identity, as follows:

1. The ethnic individual, including his or her customs, language, values, cognitions, behaviors, emotions, physical characteristics, and attitudes toward and perceptions of own and other groups.

2. Ethnic individual-intragroup relations.

3. The ethnic group, with its own characteristics, customs, language, cognitions, behaviors, emotions, and values, its enculturation of group members, provision of reflected appraisals via significant others, perceptions of ethnic membership, and attitudes and perceptions of other groups.

4. Intergroup relations, either at the group or individual level, due to the inevitable contact between the ethnic group and core group members, which can result in intergroup conflict and must lead to some form of adaptation or acculturation to each other.

5. The core or dominant group, or individual members of the group, including their intragroup socialization practices, customs, language, values, cognitions, behaviors, emotions, physical characteristics, perceptions of core group membership, and attitudes toward and perceptions of own and other groups.

6. The social context in which individuals live and interact, such as historical eras, political states, communities, and institutions.

Before proceeding to discuss the chapters, it is worth noting two things. First, the degree of explicitness of the authors' conceptualizations and/or definitions of ethnic identity varies, and second, there are differences in emphasis on the influence of the above different variables in their theories of ethnic identity. These variations seem to stem, in part, from the discipline of the authors. In the following discussion the authors' conceptualizations about the nature of ethnic identity and their definitions of ethnic identity are compared in the light of the above six sets of variables, and related to their measurement.

Theory, Definition, and Measurement.

Historian Arturo Rosales uses the term ethnic identity to refer to an ethnic class or group of people who use ethnic labels as self-identifiers. Implicit in the meaning that Rosales ascribes to ethnic identity is that people who self-identify as members of an ethnic group have an ethnic consciousness and self-awareness, as well as loyalty, and that this consciousness leads to increased loyalty when their ethnic group experiences oppression by the core society. For Rosales, ethnic self-identifiers are labels that have meanings for individuals and groups and that have been shaped by previous historical events and regional origins. Thus, Rosales' thinking about ethnic identity encompasses all six of the designated variables. In his research, he searches for evidence in the form of chronicles and oral histories that provide information about events in historical contexts, and he discusses how this evidence leads to his conclusions about the history of the ethnic identity of Mexican-origin people. He does not measure any of the variables in his conceptualization.

Anthropologist John Aguilar examines geographically-located groups of people who are defined, and define themselves, by their ethnic label, and who live either among unranked (collateral ethnicity) or ranked (stratified ethnicity) ethnic groups. Members of minority groups who live in societies that stratify ethnic groups tend to experience intergroup prejudice, discrimination, and economic exploitation. In the face of the political strife that results from stratification and exploitation, they may express their ethnicity, that is, affirm the worth and exclusiveness of their group, as part of their psychological and ideological adaptations to such adversity. Ethnic movements arise from ethnic consciousness of negative values placed by others on the group's identity; they replace these negative values with positive ones. This understanding of ethnic identity and its functions also incorporates all variables in the outline above. Aguilar does not measure ethnic identity. In his research, he makes observations and interviews ethnic group members about their ethnic group and intergroup experiences, and examines reports of similar phenomena written by other social scientists based on their own observations. There is no direct measurement of any of the variables that he uses to understand ethnic identity and ethnicity.

While the views of ethnic identity expressed by Rosales and Aguilar are different, they also are similar in that they incorporate a broad range of psychological and social variables, and they make assumptions about the meaning of the ethnic labels they use to identify their subject matter. Both of them emphasize the effects of dominant group oppression on the people who use ethnic labels, on the nature of their labels, and on their ethnic consciousness, cohesiveness, and loyalty. They attend to the identification of social events and contexts, and their effects on groups of people. They assume, but do not directly fathom, the psychological reactions of ethnic individuals or groups. Neither of them is compelled to measure aspects of the variables he studies.

Sociologist Patricia MacCorquodale conceptualizes ethnic identity at the individual level as self-categorization according to ethnic labels and the meanings associated with ethnic self-labels. These meanings include the values, symbols, and common histories that identify people as members of a distinct group. For her, ethnic identity is a social identity that is ascribed on the basis of the individual's inherited characteristics, and the traits and behaviors of members of his or her ethnic group. Ethnic identity, like other social identities, is derived from the social meanings learned through ethnic socialization, as well as through reflected appraisals from significant others and the core society. Thus, MacCorquodale's conception of ethnic identity is affected by intra and intergroup processes, thereby incorporating variables 1 through 5, but not the social context. In her chapter, she operationalizes and measures ethnic identity as self-categorization into Mexican, Mexican American, and white/Anglo. These labels or self-categorizations have considerable meaning, based on her discussion, and her data demonstrate that the labels have a strong and reliable relationship to the person's nativity, generation, and language spoken, implying a host of ethnically-based relationships, bonds, and common cultural symbols. Nevertheless, this meaning is not reflected in the simple labels she uses to measure ethnic identity, and she does not collect data on the other variables with which she understands ethnic identity.

Sociologist Leonard Gordon presents a broad conceptualization of ethnic identity as being a consequence of both intra and intergroup processes, which results in certain characteristics such as the self-perceptions and depths of meaning such perceptions have on members of the ethnic group toward their own ethnicity. In addition, he emphasizes the influence of the perceptions of members of the core society on ethnic group identity. Thus, he too touches on the same five variables that MacCorquadale incorporates in understanding ethnic identity. However, his chapter concerns the influence of dominant group members' perceptions of the ethnic group only, so he measures the assignment of positive and negative traits by mostly white college students to ethnic groups (variable 5). He does not measure any other variables, including ethnic identity.

The third sociologist, Judith Gonzalez, conceptualizes ethnic identity as a multidimensional psychological construct at the individual level, and does not dwell on its relationship to intra or intergroup relations or social context. She defines ethnic identity as including ethnic self-labeling as well as preferences for ethnic foods, language, and close friendships within one's own ethnic group. Her single measure of ethnic identity is straightforward: the reported proportion of close friends who are Mexican American and the frequency of seeking Mexican American friends to discuss personal concerns or problems.

Psychologist Kurt Organista's understanding of ethnic identity relies heavily on role/identity theory and a symbolic interactionist perspective. He views ethnic identity as one of a collection of identities, organized into a salience hierarchy, that are part of the individual's self-concept. Ethnic identity is seen as one of the most powerful identities in ethnic group members; it influences social interactions and views of the self. Identity is associated with roles that people have; thus the term role/identity, with role emphasizing a relationship to others, and identity being the internal psychological component. Because role/identities exist in relation to counter role/identities, and Organista's intent is to understand both, this conceptualization of ethnic identity incorporates the views of other ethnic and core groups, and thereby touches on the first five variables. The measurement of this notion of ethnic identity is complex, but it directly includes both ethnic and dominant group perceptions of the role/identities of the other group, as well as of their own role/identities. Thus, Organista's measure of ethnic identity directly deals with mutual perceptions on the part of ethnic and dominant groups, and targets two variables: the ethnic individual and the core group.

In their conceptualization of ethnic identity, Bernal and her colleagues, all psychologists, also view ethnic identity as a part of the self concept. They think of ethnic identity as a multidimensional construct that refers to children's perceptions that they possess characteristics and practice customs of their ethnic group, their feelings about being members of the group, and their knowledge about their ethnic group. They emphasize the influence of ethnic socialization in imparting to the developing child an understanding of the ethnic self, and of acculturation in communicating the core society's views of their ethnic group as well as the sociocultural content of that society. Thus, while they emphasize the individual's psychic self, they also consider the role played by both the ethnic group and the dominant group, and their interrelations, in shaping individual ethnic identity. As in Organista's conceptualization, they attend to the first five variables, but not to the social context, in their conceptualization. Their measurement of ethnic identity dwells on the ethnic individuals' understanding of their ethnic identity: their ethnic self-labels, ethnic self-categorization, and knowledge and use of ethnic role behaviors. They are interested in understanding the influence of the ethnic group on the children's ethnic identity. Therefore, they measure the parents' ethnic background, and assess the relationship between that background and their children's ethnic identity. Thus, they measure two variables: the individual's ethnic identity, and the ethnic group's enculturation of their children.

In summary, most of the authors discuss most of the variables that have been described as relevant to their theoretical formulations about ethnic identity. That is, they consider the ethnic individual, the relation of the individual to the ethnic group, relations between the ethnic and dominant group, and the dominant group. Historian Rosales and anthropologist Aguilar attend as well to the social context, namely, the history of the ethnic group and its region of origin, in their understanding of ethnic identity. In their measurement of variables used in conceptualizing ethnic identity, however, these social scientists differ more visibly. The differences run along disciplinary lines, with the sociologists and psychologists collecting data on ethnic identity variables, but not the historian or anthropologist.

A different dimension of difference among the authors concerns the attention they give to the measurement of individual ethnic identity. MacCorquadale and Gonzalez collect data on one dimension of individual ethnic identity, Organista gathers data on the reciprocal perceptions of ethnic and core groups by members of ethnic and core groups, and Bernal measures five different components of individual ethnic identity.

Implications and Directions for Future Research

It can be noted from the above discussion that theoretical formulations about the nature of variables implicated in the study of ethnic identity differ from the actual operationalization of an individual ethnic identity construct. In the former, investigators expound on their ideas about how ethnic identity is formed, the factors that influence it, its functions, and its complexities. In the latter, investigators seek to identify the individual's psychological experience of the state of ethnic identity, or at least to select some aspect of that experience as reflective of the state. In other words, there is a distinction being made between types of variables that are believed to have a function in the molding and understanding of ethnic identity, and the individual's psychological construction of his or her ethnic identity. The individual's ethnic identity construct may make reference to the variables that influence it, e.g., it may include the individual's sense of closeness to members of his or her ethnic group, and this feeling may have evolved from the relations between the individual and the ethnic group. However, it is the individual's feelings about the other group, not the individual's relations, that enter into the ethnic identity construct. Thus, it is important to differentiate between the construct of ethnic identity and the types of variables, listed earlier, that contribute to ethnic identity. It is also worthwhile to point out that, due to the influences of these variables, individual ethnic identity may change, i.e., it may change over time and across social contexts, as well as with exposure to different types of individual-ethnic group and ethnic-core group interactions. Because this understanding of the ethnic identity construct is at the individual level of analysis, it may be of little interest to social scientists who deal with group identities. However, to others, especially sociologists and psychologists, it may be central to their work.

Groups of people may construe their ethnic identity in a manner that is common among them. Therefore, it makes sense to speak of the ethnic identity of a group. However, such a construct would require a consensual understanding among members of that group regarding their ethnic identity, and their input into this understanding. Perhaps because of the problems inherent in the acquisition of data from defined groups, and the related issue of how the ethnic identity construction is to be assessed, social scientists have tended to identify for study individuals to whom ethnic labels have been attached. Furthermore, the use of sociodemographic categories to define ethnic groups has been criticized (McKay & Lewins, 1978). In their effort to lend clarity to the concept of ethnic group, these writers have made the distinction between ethnic category and ethnic group. In this distinction, a group is a system of interactions among people; if there is no interaction, there is no group, and one is left with an ethnic category. This ethnic category consists of an aggregate of people who are classified into specific groups because they possess characteristics such as a label, language, or nationality, but among whom there is no interaction. Along with the previous discussion, this distinction suggests that social scientists interested in studying the ethnic identity of groups need to assess the ethnic identity of individuals in a direct manner, rather than by inferring their ethnic identity on the basis of their ethnic labels or categories. McKay and Lewins (1978) further suggest that group interactions also must be assessed.

As a first step toward the advancement of knowledge about ethnic identity, the development of a commonly-accepted definition of ethnic identity is essential in the social sciences. Such a definition would have to be multidimensional, as suggested by authors of chapters in this book. This first step requires an investment of effort, since there seems to be neither a commonly-accepted definition nor agreement as to its dimensions. Furthermore, it is possible that the dimensions of ethnic identity that are relevant for children, adolescents, and adults differ or shift in importance.

A good starting point for this endeavor is the exploration of the dimension of self-identification, especially since the ethnic self-label is a widely-used index of ethnic identity, and is easy to acquire. This exploration of necessity would involve the investigation of the subjective meaning attached to ethnic labels. Identification of other dimensions, and their operationalization as measures, would allow the collection of information about their covariation, which might prove particularly interesting. As an example of the possibilities inherent in this approach, reference is made to Bernal et al's use of the ethnic identity components or dimensions of ethnic self-identification (ethnic self-labeling and self-grouping), use of ethnic behaviors, and knowledge of ethnic behaviors. It seems possible that, as ethnic knowledge wanes with generation of migration to the U. S. of an ethnic person, ethnic self-identification shifts, but ethnic preferences retain their strength and direction. Keefe and Padilla (1987)'s data on Mexican Americans in Southern California have suggested this relationship using their complex indices of ethnic awareness and ethnic loyalty: over generations, ethnic awareness decreases, but loyalty maintains. Furthermore, it is possible that this relationship is influenced by the meanings associated with the ethnic self-identification labels used.

Turning now to the variables that have been used in theoretical conceptualizations about ethnic identity, much is to be gained by planning toward the measurement of variables that play prominent roles in these conceptualizations. Once the variables are specified, amplified, and delineated, they can be operationalized and measured. The task of developing reliable and valid measures of the variables could be shared among the disciplines in order to expedite the availability of uniform measures that have good psychometric properties. These variables may be used as independent or dependent variables in research that seeks to examine them in isolation or in combination, and to elucidate their interrelationships. For example, the ethnic identity of the ethnic individual can be a dependent variable in the study of the effects of intergroup relations and core group characteristics. Similarly, ethnic identity can be the independent variable in the study of its effect upon ethnic group perceptions of and relations with the core group. A comprehensive battery for measuring aspects of each set of variables would be useful as an interdisciplinary tool in the study of ethnicity and ethnic identity. In keeping with their disciplinary and research objectives, investigators could develop and select scales for different variables from this battery to apply in their research, depending upon their particular goals, and thus facilitate the replication of research. Ultimately, these efforts could lead to theoretical views and models of ethnic identity that could be assessed for their validity across ethnic groups.

The availability of a uniform index of ethnic identity, and a theoretical framework that is generalizable across ethnic groups, has a number of implications worth noting. In order to evaluate the impact of acculturation on new immigrants, it is essential to have a baseline of their ethnic identity. Changes that occur due to influences of the core society, including those due to exogamy, social class shifts, and political movements, can be assessed best by studying ethnic identity status at entry into a society. There also are a number of practical applications of such an index and theoretical framework. As noted by some of the authors of the chapters in this book, ethnic identity has been viewed as a key variable in a number of areas, including aspects of behavior and psychological adjustment, health and mental health, family relationships, political movements and actions, and voting patterns.

The richness of theoretical views of ethnic identity, coupled with the restrained measurement of one, and seldom more, dimensions of ethnic identity in the current literature, suggests that there is much about this topic that has not been explored. It has been the intent of this book to provide some direction and impetus to that exploration.

References

Aguilar, J. L. (1992). Expressive ethnicity and ethnic identity in Mexican and Mexican America. In M. E. Bernal & P. C. Martinelli (Eds.), <u>Mexican American identity</u>. Encino, CA: Floricanto Press.

Bernal, M. E., Knight, G. P., Organista, K. C., Garza, C. A., & Maez, B. M. (1992). In M. E. Bernal & P. C. Martinelli (Eds.), <u>Mexican American identity</u>. Encino, CA: Floricanto Press.

Gonzalez, J. T. (1992). Dilemmas of the high achieving Chicana: The double-bind factor in male/female relationships. In M. E. Bernal & P. C. Martinelli (Eds.), <u>Mexican American identity</u>. Encino, CA: Floricanto Press.

Gordon, L. (1992). College student perceptions of ethnic identity: The case of Mexican Americans. In M. E. Bernal & P. C. Martinelli (Eds.), <u>Mexican American identity</u>. Encino, CA: Floricanto Press.

Keefe, S. E., & Padilla, A. M. (1987). <u>Chicano ethnicity.</u> Albuquerque, NM: University of New Mexico Press.

MacCorquodale, P. (1992). Identity: Gender and ethnic dimensions. In M. E. Bernal & P. C. Martinelli (Eds.), <u>Mexican American identity</u>. Encino, CA: Floricanto Press.

Martinelli, P. C. (1992). Mexican American identity: An interdisciplinary approach. In M. E. Bernal & P. C. Martinelli (Eds.), <u>Mexican American identity</u>. Encino, CA: Floricanto Press.

McKay, J., & Lewins, F. (1978). Ethnicity and the ethnic group: A conceptual analysis and reformulation. <u>Ethnic and Racial Studies, 1</u>, 412-427.

Organista, K. C. (1992). Use of the role/identity procedure for assessing ethnic identity in Mexican American high school students. In M. E. Bernal & P. C. Martinelli, <u>Mexican American identity</u>. Encino, CA: Floricanto Press.

Rosales, F. A. (1992). Mexican immigrant nationalism as an origin of identity for Mexican Americans: Exploring the sources. In M. E. Bernal & P. C. Martinelli (Eds.), <u>Mexican American identity</u>. Encino, CA: Floricanto Press.

Printed in the United States
140231LV00003B/33/A